PALOMAS MTNS.

Gila *River*

Sentinel

84 106

Aztec

8

Dateland

Malpais
lava badlands
(Death trap)

46

...and Tank Wash

8

115 101

102

117 73

72A AGUILA MTNS.

123

121E

San Cristobal

60 93

92

96

Rat Gap

48

Eagle Tanks

BARRY M. GOLDWATER
AIR FORCE RANGE

CRATER MTNS.

Tenmile Wash

49

5

138

Water 133

Black Tanks
(Hohokam
water holes)

159

29

85

SAUCEDA
MOUNTAINS

SAUCEDA MOUNTAUNS

175

151

174

173

167

172

Game Tanks

MOUNTAINS

Mohawk Wash

3

SIERRA

PINTA

DESERT

Heart Tank

Pinta
Sands

13

27

O'Neill's
grave

103

9E

Nameer 1871
18

Las Playas

41

33

32

Papago
Well

Jabonero
15

57

148

SIERRA
DEL PINACATE

nacate
va Flow

GRANITE MTNS.

Red Point
(live-fire area)

Wash

Growler

BRYAN MTNS.

GROWLER MOUNTAINS

Daniels

Arroyo

Wash

Hohokam

24

131A

131D

131C

AGUA
DULCE
MOUNTAINS

26

23

137

Quitobaquito
Springs

2

Mexico

CHILDS
MTN.

51

166

122

Ajo

156

Charlie Bell
Well

Bates
Well

35

Cuerda de Leña Wash

Kino
Peak

BATES MOUNTAINS

52

Dripping
Springs

85

25

La Abra
Plain

11

39

Sonoyta

3

8

2

BATAMOTE
MTNS.

Why

160

86

ORGAN PIPE CACTUS
NATIONAL MONUMENT

10B

168

44

170

Lukeville

1

SIKORT
CHUAPO
MTNS.

TOHONO
O'ODHAM
INDIAN
RESERVATION

AJO RANGE

Sweetwater
Pass

UNITED STATES
MEXICO

36

142

171

141

154

140

153

139

149

109

144

136

155

135

147

150

157

143

162

163

CABEZA PRIETA
NATIONAL
WILDLIFE REFUGE

DEAD IN THEIR TRACKS

✝ ✝ ✝
✝ ✝
✝

Also by John Annerino

DEAD IN THEIR TRACKS

TRACKS

Crossing America's Desert Borderlands

John Annerino

With photographs and maps by the author.

FOUR WALLS EIGHT WINDOWS
NEW YORK † LONDON

© 1999 John Annerino
Photographs ©, maps © 1999 John Annerino

Published in the United States by:

Four Walls Eight Windows
39 West 14th Street, room 503
New York, N.Y., 10011

U.K. offices:
Four Walls Eight Windows/Turnaround
Unit 3, Olympia Trading Estate
Coburg Road, Wood Green
London N22 6TZ, England

Visit our website at http://www.fourwallseightwindows.com

First printing April 1999.

Photographs on pps. 64, 130, and 131 by David F. Roberson, from the collection of the author.

Library of Congress Cataloging-in-Publication Data:

Annerino, John .
    Dead in Their Tracks: Crossing America's Desert Borderlands/
      by John Annerino.
        p.   cm.
    Includes bibliographical references and index.
    ISBN 1-56858-132-7
      1. U.S.-Mexico Border Region—Description and travel. 2. Arizona—
Description and travel. 3. Annerino, John—Journeys—U.S.-Mexico Border
Region. 4. Annerino, John—Journeys—Arizona. 5. United States—Emigration
and immigration. 6. Mexico—Emigration and immigration. 7. Immigrants—
U.S.-Mexico Border Region—History. 8. Pioneers—U.S.-Mexico Border
Region—History. 9. U.S. Border Patrol—History.
      I. Title.
    F786.A57 1999   99-21341
    917.904'33—dc21   CIP

Photography layout and design by John Annerino
Maps designed by Gus Walker
Book design by Terry Bain

10 9 8 7 6 5 4 3 2 1
Printed in the United States

Cover photograph by John Annerino/Gamma-Liaison

"The future always looks good in the golden land because nobody remembers the past."

Joan Didion
Some Dreamers of the Golden Dream

The forlorn sweep of the Mohawk Sand Dunes is a death trap that has claimed the lives of many Mexican nationals who've vanished in the drifting sands.

CONTENTS

LIST OF MAPS

ACKNOWLEDGMENTS

Encouragment and support for this book came from many photography editors, associates, friends, loved ones, and others who remain unnamed behind the scenes—and to them I am endebted for keeping this project alive throughout the long, hot decade it took to complete it: Guy Cooper at *Newsweek*, Peter Howe while at *Life*, Jennifer B. Coley while at the Gamma-Liaison photo agency, the late Richard S. Vonnier at *Phoenix*, Stephanie Robertson while at *The Arizona Republic*, Paul Schatt, and Joseph C. Wilder at *The Journal of the Southwest*. I am also indebted to retired *Life* picture editor Melvin L. Scott, and to Bill Broyles. Their enthusiasm for the importance of this story never waned. I am grateful for the help of Donnamarie Barnes at Liaison International, Frank Orozco, Norma Lebario, Lucinda Bush, Mary García, private investigator Joseph P. Berumi, Gus Walker, and Terry Bain. Portions of this book would not have been possible without the help of ret. Major Bruce Lohman USMC, the late Border Patrol pilot David F. Roberson, and retired Border Patrol tracker Joe M. McCraw. Nor would this work have been completed without the kind Mexican citizens who opened their homes to me, and the unfailing belief and love of my wife Alejandrina. Yet, were it not for the convictions of publisher John G.H. Oakes, you would not be holding this book in your hands on the eve of the American borderlands' next "season of death."

The ancient desert paths of the Sand Pápago were followed by Mexican gold seekers during the 1850s California gold rush.

To the brave men, women and children who died in search of the American dream. To the desperate political refugees who fled violence and oppression. To the dedicated Border Patrol pilots and trackers who tried to save them. And to many others we'll never know.

Border Phantoms.

The lure of distant American cities like Phoenix leads many immigrants to attempt crossing the desert borderlands on foot.

"The road is my road,
the road of summer.
And I'm a vagabond,
traveling in this world."

El Camino
The Gypsy Kings

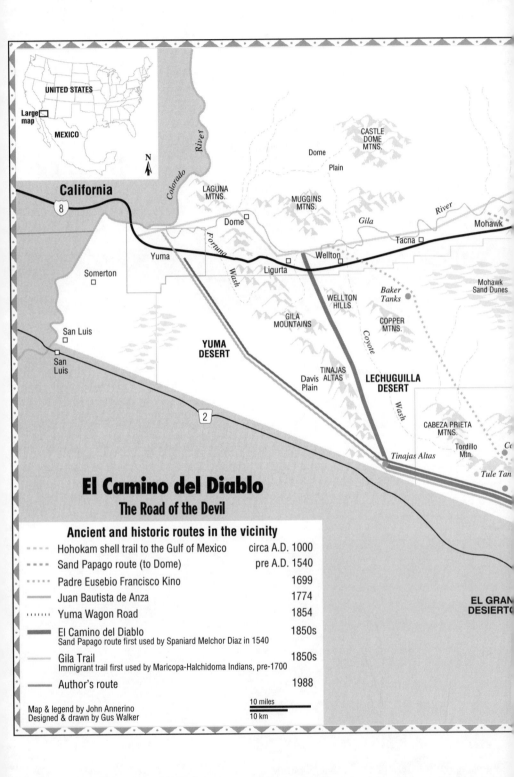

UNITED STATES

Large map

MEXICO

N

California

8

Colorado River

Fortuna Wash

LAGUNA MTNS.

Dome

Dome Plain

CASTLE DOME MTNS.

MUGGINS MTNS.

Gila

River

Mohawk

Tacna

Yuma

Wellton

Somerton

Ligurta

WELLTON HILLS

Baker Tanks

Mohawk Sand Dunes

San Luis

GILA MOUNTAINS

COPPER MTNS.

Coyote

San Luis

YUMA DESERT

TINAJAS ALTAS

Davis Plain

LECHUGUILLA DESERT

2

Wash

CABEZA PRIETA MTNS.

Tordillo Mtn.

Ce

Tinajas Altas

Tule Tan

El Camino del Diablo
The Road of the Devil

Ancient and historic routes in the vicinity

- - - - Hohokam shell trail to the Gulf of Mexico   circa A.D. 1000

- - - - Sand Papago route (to Dome)   pre A.D. 1540

· · · · · Padre Eusebio Francisco Kino   1699

——— Juan Bautista de Anza   1774

· · · · · · Yuma Wagon Road   1854

——— El Camino del Diablo   1850s
Sand Papago route first used by Spaniard Melchor Diaz in 1540

——— Gila Trail   1850s
Immigrant trail first used by Maricopa-Halchidoma Indians, pre-1700

——— Author's route   1988

Map & legend by John Annerino
Designed & drawn by Gus Walker

10 miles
10 km

EL GRAN
DESIERTO

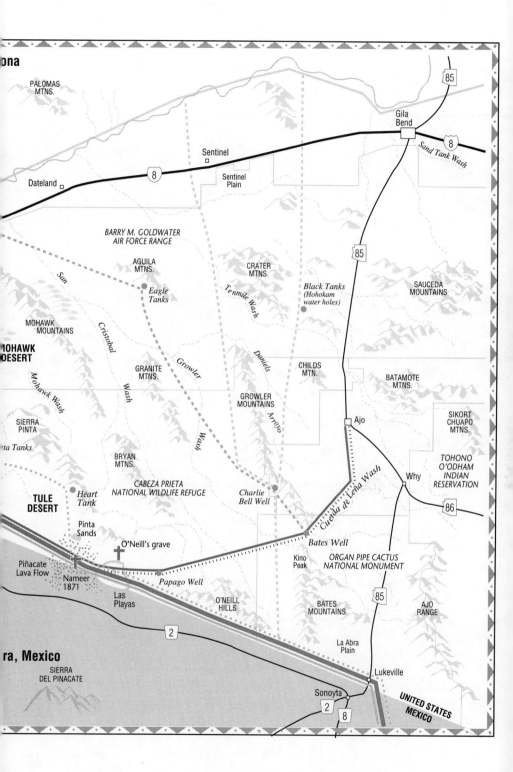

Bruce Lohman (left) and Dave Roberson walk past Nameer's grave on the third day of what, in modern times, was an unprecedented 130-mile long, six-day mid-summer trek across the Camino del Diablo.

† 1 †

THE ROAD OF THE DEVIL

†

"The Tinajas was a vast graveyard of unknown dead . . .
the scattered bones of human beings slowly turning to
dust . . . the dead were left where they were to be sepulchered
by the fearful sand storms that sweep at times over the
desolate waste."

Don Francisco Salazar, 1850
on the Camino del Diablo

DUST DEVILS whirl around us as the raw sun torches the
bleak landscape. The hot sand blisters our feet. The vast
desert swallows our footsteps. And the distant mirages consume our dreams.

We plod on, breathing in the scorched air of the morning sun. The
wet bandanas covering our mouths do little to soothe our parched
throats. And the hot water steaming in our plastic jugs does little to
slake our incurable thirst.

Yet every ten to fifteen minutes I stop and force myself to choke
down a mouthful or two of the putrid liquid. And each time the hot water
washes across my stomach I gag. But it is the only way to stave off
dehydration and death in the merciless Lechuguilla Desert.

For the last five days I've coaxed my two companions to do the same.
And now that we've entered the heart of this killing ground, I'm berat-
ing them to guzzle their water as well. But they will have none of it.
Fatigue and heat stress have fogged their thinking. And they insist on sip-
ping and saving their water, even as they fall further and further behind.

Dave is the first to go down, staggering then collapsing in the hot white sand that sears his sunburned legs and hands. So Bruce and I guide him into the shade of a mesquite tree in the lonely reaches of Coyote Wash. We peel off Dave's heavy pack, and his bloodshot eyes roll back behind the scratched lenses of his glasses. I clutch Dave's limp arm and check his pulse; it is racing at 120 beats a minute. Bruce's pulse is 80 beats a minute; he is still sweating, but he's already got that unmistakable 'forty-mile stare.' My pulse is fifty beats a minute; I'm hot, but I still feel coherent. Thus triaged, Bruce and I ply Dave with water and swath his head, face, and neck with wet bandanas. When Dave finally comes around, he agrees to guzzle his water.

A half-hour later we are on the move again, following *El Camino del Diablo* (The Road of the Devil), toward the hardrock spine of the Tinajas Altas Mountains: At 2,764-feet, the raw bones of the 230 million-year-old sierra erupt out of the floor of this forbidding tract of lower Sonoran Desert. Yet, hidden within its barranca of white stone, *Tinajas Altas* (high tanks), has always held the promise of life for those who'd been forced to cross the Devil's Road. We are close, no more than five miles from those life-saving waterholes. But people rarely died in the middle of this desert; death usually rattled within grasp of the ancient tinajas.

I turn around to check my companions' progress again; Dave is marching confidently, but Bruce is starting to falter.

"Bruce! Are you okay?" I stop and ask.

Without missing a footstep, he starts vomiting. "Yeah, fine," he says, wiping the vile spew off his chin with his bare hand. His eyes look like they've sunken in the back of his head, but he keeps walking, then stumbles. The white sun is burning across our desolate path, and gusts of stinging sand rake our dry skin when Bruce goes down.

This odyssey began five days ago, not far from where José Hernández found a body hanging by a belt from a tree. Empty plastic water jugs lay scattered at the dead man's feet, as his bloated corpse swung back and forth in the hot wind. José was headed north to work—a dangerous hundred-mile desert trek he's made from Sonoyta, Sonora to Gila Bend, Arizona four consecutive summers—when he stumbled upon the grisly death scene of his fellow countryman. Suicide has sometimes been the only escape for those suffering from the ravages of death by dehydration in America's killing ground.

The three of us, however, were headed 130 miles west from Ajo to Yuma, Arizona along the Camino del Diablo; it was the first time any of us had undertaken this dangerous journey, but we each had what we felt were justifiable reasons for crossing the infamous Camino del Diablo. Bruce Lohman was a retired Marine major and helicopter pilot, and Dave Roberson was a Border Patrol tracker and fixed-wing pilot. Both had flown extensively throughout the region and both were drawn to face the hazards of crossing the Camino del Diablo on foot during the raging heat of summer. For myself, it was a combination of factors having to do with walking a mile in someone else's footsteps.

During the previous decade, I'd traced many of Arizona's historic trails and prehistoric routes on foot—including its southern borderlands—simply because there were questions that couldn't be answered and experiences that couldn't be had from behind the security and comfort of a desk. The Camino del Diablo was particularly mystifying to me. Since its first recorded crossing in 1540 up to the present day it earned a reputation as the deadliest immigrant trail in North America, and its historic deathtoll tragically coalesced with the grim tally wrought by the modern immigrant routes that now criss-cross it. I'd already struggled across this same desert during the fearsome heat of August with Mexican citizens; so I knew I would also have to cross the Camino del Diablo during the blazing summer months in order to compare the routes, see what answers might unveil themselves along the way, and what perceptions might be gleaned from our deadly immigration policy.

But crossing the Camino del Diablo has never been easy.

Bordered on the north by the phantom course of the Gila River, on the west by the forlorn sweep of the Colorado and Mojave Deserts, on the east by the ancestral Sonoran Desert lands of the Pápago, and on the south by Sonora, Mexico's daunting *Gran Desierto*, the southwest corner of Arizona's borderlands comprises a 4,100 square mile no-man's land that Spanish conquistadors feared as a *despoblado* (uninhabited land). Cleaved by the serrated crests of seventeen basin and range-type mountain ranges, and guarded by the harsh sands, sweeping bajadas, and black malpaís of the Yuma, Tule, and Lechuguilla deserts, this forbidding region comprised the ancestral lands of the *Hía Ced O'odham* (People of the Sand), band of Pápago. One of the only trails that immigrants used to traverse the Sand Pápago's haunting domain was the 130-mile long Camino del Diablo. The Camino del Diablo traced the ancient tracks of this aboriginal band of intrepid hunters and gatherers who forged a desert path from one distant waterhole to the next. But this austere desert region proved too hostile even for the native Sand Pápago. Forcefully displaced from their vast homelands by Mexican soldiers for preying on California bound immigrants and prospectors during the 1850s, their fate was sealed with the creation of Organ Pipe Cactus National Monument in 1937, the Cabeza Prieta National Wildlife Refuge in 1939, and the Luke Air Force Range in 1941. The Sand Pápago marched into cultural extinction after nearly a millennium of eking out a desperate existence in one of the driest and most forbidding desert regions in North America.

Crossed in 1540 by Spaniard Melchior Díaz who was under orders from conquistador Francisco Vásquez de Coronado to rendezvous with Capt. Juan Hernando de Alarcón near the Colorado River delta, the Camino del Diablo was later traversed by a succession of Spanish explorers and missionaries, including Padre Eusebio Francisco Kino who crossed it on three separate occasions while mapping the region between 1698 and 1701, and Padre Francisco Tomás Garcés who made the first mid-summer crossing of the Camino in 1779 in hopes of establishing a mission on the Colorado River. It was the forty-niners, however, who later followed in the footsteps of the tireless padres, who fared even worse than the indigenous Sand Pápago. Historians believe that between the 1850s and the turn of the century, four hundred to two thousand gold seekers—many of them Mexican nationals—died of thirst in this unforgiving corner of New Mexico and Arizona territory.

Tragically, the forty-niners were not the last to succumb to slow death by dehydration in this historic killing ground. With the end of the Bracero Program in 1964, a wave of undocumented workers from Mexico risked apprehension and deportation in order to continue seeking their dreams in America's modern goldfields. Those who attempted crossing the U.S./Mexico border through the cruel desert many cursed as *El Sahuaro* including myriad Central American refugees risked losing the greatest treasure of them all.

It is August 22, and the pink sun is burning through the dawn cloud cover when the three of us leave Highway 85 south of Ajo and start down the Yuma Wagon Road leg of the Camino del Diablo. We are carrying a week's supply of rations, three gallons of water each, and extra empty plastic water jugs. The gnats are voracious, and crushing them between my fingertips does little to stop the black swarms from whining in my ears, eyes, and nose. Worse, the humidity is appalling, and I'm overcome with crotch rot the first few hours out; so I'm forced to don a loincloth hastily made from a torn cotton t-shirt. Our first camp is at Bates Well, seventeen miles out, across the saguaro and mesquite-covered plains of the Valley of the Ajo.

The grasshoppers are buzzing and the smell of greasewood permeates the muggy air when we reach Bates Well in Organ Pipe Cactus National Monument at 2:40 PM. It's 106 degrees in the shade, we are weary and footsore, but we've made it to the first waterhole in a low rocky pass between the Bates Mountains and the Growler Mountains.

First used by the Sand Pápago who called it *Tjunikáatk* (Where There Is Saguaro), for the bountiful harvest of sweet red cactus fruit they collected here each June, Bates Well was later inhabited by Henry Gray. Until his death in 1976, the steely-eyed pioneer stockman maintained his right to run cattle where park service bureaucrats preferred to count tourists. The first of six principal immigration routes crosses the Camino del Diablo at Bates Well, and the wily half-deaf old caretaker, told me he long made the practice of leaving out a five-gallon jug of water for desperate travelers striking out from Sonoyta, Sonora to Ajo and beyond to Gila Bend. It is a tortuous, unmarked hundred-mile journey that would test the will and stamina of most professional athletes. On July 2, 1980, thirty-one Salvadorans crossed the wire seperating Organ Pipe Cactus National Monument from the frontier of Sonora and unwittingly embarked upon a death march that cost them $2,500 each, led by Salvadoran and Mexican *coyotes* (smugglers). Ill-prepared for the horrible saga that unfolded, most carried little more than a gallon of water each, and tragically none ever made it any where near Bates Well.* In the two days and nights that followed, fourteen people were rescued from the throes of death by Border Patrol trackers and U.S. Customs agents, while thirteen of their companions died miserably after failing to slake their thirst with perfume and urine.** Two others were never found, and one *coyote* escaped.

The stark black ridges of 3,197-foot Kino Peak pierce the titian mist of the setting sun when Dave, Bruce and I finish topping off with six gallons of water each at Bates Well. Monsoon rains hammer the Pápago desert borderlands far to the east, but dreamy cascades of orange *virga* fail to slake the parched ground of the Devil's Road to the west. It is an omen of what awaits us beyond. I bed down on the hard desert floor, pull a white cotton sheet over my face, and listen to mosquitos hunt for exposed flesh throughout the long, hot night.

By six the next morning, we are striding through an unremitting sweep of creosote flats when Dave suddenly yells at me from behind: "Look what you just stepped over!" Coiled in the coarse sand next to my footprint is a Mojave rattlesnake. One hit from a horned sidewinder's deadly neurotoxin and, for those who are lucky enough to survive, terrible lifelong scars are inflicted. I slowly step away, changing a camera lens as I do, and the sidewinder strikes. In the wink of an eye, it whirls out of its crater and snaps at the hot air a yard in front of me.

First used in 1854 to haul rich copper ore from the Ajo mines to Yuma, the desolate stretch of the Yuma Wagon Road we are following was also used by *narcotraficantes* (drug smugglers), before passage of the North American Free Trade Agreement in 1994 opened the floodgates to Mexico's fifteen to thirty billion dollars commerce of profit and death. Under the cover of darkness, loads of *mota* (marijuana), grown in Mexico's Sierra Madre Occidental, *goma* (heroin), harvested from the

* (See Appendix B: "Water Requirements for Crossing America's Killing Ground.")
** (See Appendix C: "Desert Rescues.")

neighboring golden triangle region of Durango, Sinaloa, and Chihuahua, and *cocaína* (cocaine) airlifted from distant Colombia, were run north from Sonora's Highway 2. The route continued along the western border of Organ Pipe Cactus National Monument, and the desolate backroads of the Pápago Indian Reservation, into Phoenix.

We follow in this deep sandy track as it probes the desert to the west. And by the time we reach the barbed wire fence separating Organ Pipe from the Cabeza Prieta National Wildlife Refuge and the Barry M. Goldwater Range, we've hot-footed around three more sidewinders. They are the main reason I refused to trek the Camino del Diablo during cooler nighttime hours; they're difficult to see coiled in the sand by day—they'd be impossible to see in the dark. When Olga Wright Smith prospected the distant Copper Mountains during the 1930s with her husband Cap and his father Old Cap, she wrote: "There was so many rattlers them days that men . . . had to wear stove pipes on their laigs to keep from gettin' bit. An' the rattlers strikin' agin' them stovepipes sounded like hail on a tin roof."

Follow the Organ Pipe fenceline north, one source told me, and a second body could be found hanging in a tree. It was something I promised myself I would do: say a prayer for the departed, and record the tragic passing of yet another brave, desperate soul who died far from home in search of a better life. But I was new to photographing the skeletal remains of Mexican citizens, and I wasn't sure how I would react—miles from nowhere—at the sight of a black corpse swinging in the wind. Assuming I succeeded in locating it.

We push on into the searing maw of the Growler Valley. An ancient travel corridor used by the Hohokam people circa A.D. 1000, they wandered this virtually waterless blast of desert from the Salt and Gila Rivers 150 to 200 miles south to the Gulf of California in their ritual quest for blue glycymeris shells they fashioned into sacred pendants and jewelry. Today, another modern immigration route crosses the Camino del Diablo in this sprawling desert valley and follows the ancient path of the Hohokam through an active bombing zone in the Barry M. Goldwater Range. But it is a desert journey far beyond the reach of most people. I peer north into that unimaginable distance and what shimmers in the heat waves dancing on the horizonline is the haunting mirage of fourteen men lying in the shade of an ironwood tree. No one has ever found them, but they are still out there, their rubber soles curling off their bony feet, their cracked plastic water jugs filling with sand, their leather scalps peeling back from their white skulls, the wallet-sized smiles of their loved ones turning brittle in their gnarled black hands. In the Piman language, *hohokam* is said to mean "those who have vanished." And on the forlorn western flanks of the 3,029-foot Growler Mountains pictographs of sea shells still mark the ancient Hohokam waterhole those desperate men almost reached. But, like the Hohokam, they too have vanished— and no one knows who they were, where they came from, or what words passed from their lips before they all perished.

Follow the arc of the Sand Pápago trail northwest from Bates Well 110 miles across the desert to Dome, on what was believed to be a three-day journey for Arizona's ancient Bedouins. Beyond the mass grave of the "vanished ones," the scattered sun-bleached bones of at least a dozen other men are said to be slowly turning to dust in the black lava of the 1,800-foot Aguila Mountains. A legend, some say; "another wetback story," others insist. But you need only imagine the Salvadoran tragedy out here in this fearful expanse of no-man's land and who would have ever found them, or even known they walked off the face of the earth in search of the "golden land"?

Someday, I promised myself, I would look for their remains, too, and add their haunting images to the venerable list of honest men who disappeared in their dire search for the American dream. But reports keep surfacing. The death toll never stops mounting.* And the illusory phantoms become impossible to track down alone on foot in a killing ground that runs to the horizon in every direction.

In practical terms, crossing the historic Camino del Diablo has always been a question of math and endurance. Can you carry enough water, whether traveling by foot, horseback, or wagon, to reach the next waterhole? And what are you going to do if that waterhole is dry? The math for the Camino del Diablo is simple enough: of one-hundred-twenty-eight waterholes that have been recorded in this Empty Quarter of Arizona and northwest Sonora's *Gran Desierto*—including *tinajas* (rock tanks), *charcos* (mud holes), springs, and manmade tanks that have been specially built for desert bighorn sheep and Sonoran pronghorn antelope—only six waterholes lie along the route we are following. Compound this paucity of waterholes, with the mileage between them—17, 23, 31, 3, 17, and 40—and you have the conditions for the endless series of tragedies that contributed to the Camino del Diablo's heinous reputation. Many early immigrants, however, struck out along the Camino del Diablo during summer monsoons—as we had. They thought they would find pools of rainwater between distant waterholes that would provide some margin of safety not even the 1854 Texas Railroad survey crews had when they traversed the region during the cloudless blistering month of June.

By the time we reach San Cristóbal Wash, we know our monsoon timing will pay off for us as well. Standing water, hip-deep, stretches a

---

* (On Friday, September 4, 1998, Border Patrol pilot Howard Aitken found the body of a Mexican national four miles north of the U.S./Mexico border on the west end of Arizona's 1,169-foot Butler Mountains. Aitken estimates the body had been there for approximately three weeks).

The gnarled black hand of a modern Mexican immigrant who perished crossing the the Camino del Diablo's historic killing ground.

hundred yards in front of us. Bruce opts for the dry ground, but Dave and I wade through the hot, stagnant pool of brown water bantering "We *swam* to Yuma." We break for lunch and lie-up out of the noonday sun in the sparse shade of a dry arroyo.

The clock is ticking, our water is dwindling, and two hours later we are headed toward Pápago Well when I stumble. My head is spinning, my stomach is reeling, and I go down; I crawl on all fours through the hot sand into the lean shade of a creosote bush and curl up in a fetal position gasping. Dave and Bruce stare down at me. "We didn't figure on anything happening to you," they tell me.

"Must have been that second can of sardines," I groan. "Just give me a few minutes."

An hour of moaning and shivering in the hot sun, the bug passes and the water revives me. We start walking again, when six Sonoran pronghorn antelope scatter like ghosts through the greasewood and ocotillo near the Pápago Well's trail fork. It starts raining and lightning rumbles out of the opal-blue thunderheads towering over Chinaman's Flat. But we are the high ground, so we drop spread-eagle on the desert pavement until the lightning passes. We stagger around the northern flanks of the 2,850-foot Sierra Agua Dulce (Sweet Water Mountains) and arrive at Pápago Well in a cool drizzle at 8:30 PM.

Unlike the relic Sand Pápago waterholes of Tule Tank and Tinajas Altas, the 235-foot deep Pápago Well did not exist in the heyday of the forty-niners; it was drilled some time before 1909 to furnish the nearby Pápago and Legal Tender mines. So anyone who traveled the ancient Camino del Diablo, or Yuma Wagon Road, before then had to make the sixty-five- or seventy-five-mile pull into Tule Tank—or die trying. Even with the relative advantage of Pápago Well, however, on Day 3 we are moving by 5:15 AM; we are carrying five gallons of water each to reach Tule Well thirty-one miles west. It is a long and dangerous pull through one of the bleakest stretches of the Camino del Diablo, and fear of not being able to cover that harsh empty ground drives us silently on toward the daunting inferno that awaits us in the Pinta Sands and Pinacate Lava Flow. At Mile 44 (from Ajo), we stop at the grave of prospector Dave O'Neill; some believe O'Neill drowned in 1916 after he fell down drunk. Others, like geologist Kirk Bryan, who surveyed this desolate region in 1917 for his U.S. Geological Survey water-supply paper *Routes to Desert Watering Places in Pápago Country: Arizona*, attributed his death to exposure and overexertion: "His burros wandered away from his camp in a storm," wrote Bryan, "and after searching for them for at least a day, he [O'Neill] died with his head in a mudhole." A grim reminder on this frightful day, O'Neill's death has been an omen for Mexican citizens who drown in the swift moving Mohawk Canal *after* surviving the punishing Lechuguilla Desert crossing to the west.

In the bone-white dry lake bed of Las Playas, the Yuma Wagon Road links up with the ancient Camino del Diablo; we start down this leg of the Camino del Diablo and head northwest toward the Tinajas Altas Mountains where we plan to connect with Juan Bautista de Anza's two hundred-year-old route to cross the Yuma Desert. But standing between us and Tule Well, the next waterhole, is the smothering sweep of the Pinta Sands and the rugged black *malpaís* (badlands) of the Pinacate Lava Flow. The air temperature is hovering around 110 degrees in the shade—but there is no shade. The ground temperature is pushing 160 degrees Fahrenheit. We are losing moisture through respiration, perspiration, and conduction, and as much as we want this obstacle at our backs, we can't drink water fast enough to keep walking through the furnace heat. We scurry into the thin shade of several large creosote bushes and lay-up on the skin-burning black lava west of Las Playas.

All variations of the Camino del Diablo passed through Las Playas simply because it was the most reliable ephemeral water source between Quitobaquito Springs thirty-miles southeast and Tinajas Altas forty-two miles northwest. Monsoon rains frequently turned the dry lake into a glimmering sea of life for those on the verge of death. During his July, 1861 crossing of the Camino del Diablo, Harvard professor Raphael Pumpelly and five companions were trying to outride a dozen "cutthroats" from Old Mexico when they went down at Las Playas. Camped on the edge of this dry pan of sun-cracked clay without water, Pumpelly reported temperatures between 118-126 degrees in the shade and 160 degrees in the direct sunlight. Fortunately for Pumpelly's outfit, it stormed during the night, and he was able to write of that providential rain later: "A broad sheet of water, only a few inches deep, covered the playas for miles before us, and banished from our minds all fear of suffering."

The forlorn gravestones that line our treacherous path through the suffocating heat of the Pinta Sands and the Pinacate Lava Flow are testimony to those who weren't as fortunate as Pumpelly. And none is more mysterious than Nameer's grave. His intaglio-sized headstone sits out in the middle of the burning black lava and in bold stone letters reads: NAMEER 1871. Like so many others who continue to vanish in the Camino's carnivorous heat, no one—so far as is known—has discovered who Nameer was.

One hundred twenty-four years later, Miguel Soto and his companion crossed the border near Nameer's grave and stumbled upon a scene of death in the seething wastes north of here he would never forget: "There was a woman, an El Salvadoran woman, I remembered seeing a few weeks before in Mexico," Soto reported. "She was clutching a five- or six-year old girl in her arms. A few feet away was another little girl, about the same age. She, too, was dead. Nearby we saw a

Used for aerial target practice on the Barry M. Goldwater Range, a military tow dart lays buried nose-down in the Pinta Sands.

teenage girl. She, too, was dead. And about fifty feet away was another dead teenage girl." Five days later Border Patrol trackers found the fifth victim, another woman, but coyotes had reached her first and eaten her left leg.

The Camino is an endless struggle of will for us, and it takes everything we can muster to cross the firey Tule Desert and reach Tule Well in the dark, shattered lowlands between the Tule Mountains and the Cabeza Prieta Mountains by 1:00 AM.

Day 4 is our scheduled rest day, and we hole up in the shade of Tule Well throughout the day, tending to blisters, sore muscles, heat stress, and sleep deprivation. Like Pápago Well, Tule Well was not a reality during the gold rushes of the 1850s and 1860s, when the Camino del Diablo bore the traffic of thousands. In his history of Sonora, *Noticías Estadísticas del Estado de Sonora, 1850*, José Francisco Velasco estimated that between five and six thousand people left Hermosillo, Sonora for the California goldfields between October, 1848 and March, 1849. Nobody knows how many thousands joined the exodus in the decade that followed, but as early as 1849 thirteen thousand of the estimated one hundred thousand non-Indians living in California were Mexican citizens. One can only speculate how many *Californios* perished on the Camino del Diablo en route. One man who did not was Don Francisco Salazar; he left Hermosillo at the age of seventeen, crossed the Camino del Diablo on foot in the spring of 1850 with a party of twenty men, and reached the rich placers of Hangtown in California's Sierra Nevada more than a thousand hard miles north in September. The Mexicans proved to be such good miners they incurred the wrath and prejudice of American miners unfamiliar with the Sonoran's tried and true mining methods of using *arrastras* for crushing ore, digging "coyote tunnels" to locate hidden veins, and using mercury to separate the gold. After a year of toiling in the goldfields, Don Francisco Salazar rode horseback, via the small Mexican settlement of Nuestra de Señora de Los Ángeles, back to Hermosillo carrying $50,000 in gold; Salazar reportedly used his share of the mother lode to buy a sugar plantation, but his story proved to be one of the Camino del Diablo's rare happy ones.

Yet another Mexican citizen who died tragically was dumped into Tule Well. Dug sometime before the 1893 International Boundary Survey, Tule Well's foul tasting sulphur-laden water was legendary; an enterprising, unidentified Mexican man reportedly sold water here until he was shot dead by a poor thirsty customer. Raphael Pumpelly wrote of the incident after his 1915 Model T expedition along the Camino del Diablo. A friend had asked Pumpelly how he liked the water at Tule Well.

"Not much," Pumpelly answered.

"Naturally," the friend said, "for we found and left a man in it two years ago."

At 5:00 PM, we saunter three miles down to Tule Tank, an ancient Sand Pápago encampment called *Ótoxakam* (Where There Is Bulrush). This shallow tinaja was a pivotal, though not always dependable, water stop for thirst-ravaged travelers on the Camino del Diablo; those who pulled out damp sand where they'd envisioned cool spring water were forced to struggle another seventeen miles west across the sun-scorched Lechuguilla Desert to Tinajas Altas. Many did not make it. We bed down on the desert pavement near this ancient waterhole in hopes of making an early morning dash to Tinajas Altas, over the horizon.

Carrying three gallons of water each, we roll at dawn, and march briskly beneath the rocky, pinto-colored flanks of 2,107-foot Tordillo Mountain. Little more than two hours out, we stop at a thirty-foot circle of rocks known as the Circle-of-8. In 1896, Capt. David DuBose Gaillard of the International Boundary Commission wrote it was the scene of one of the "most pathetic cases of death from thirst" in the long, tragic history of the Camino del Diablo. In *The Perils and Wonders of a True Desert*, Capt. Gaillard reported that a Mexican family of eight was forced to stop in the middle of the Lechuguilla Desert when their team of horses gave out. While unloading their wagon, their water container, a wickerwork stoneware demijohn, fell, broke, and sealed the fate of the entire family. More recent reports by the late pioneer Arizonan Tom Childs, however, indicate the family was murdered by the Sand Pápago. When Childs visited the site with two Sand Pápago in 1884, he asked them how the family died. "We killed them," they told him, "for their loot." Childs wrote, "When I pressed them for further details, they explained that they obtained some tobacco and other things, including some buckskin bags with gold in them. They said they had no use for the gold, so they emptied it among the greasewood bushes, but kept the bags, which they could use." One of the most pressing reasons immigrants and forty-niners followed the dangerous border route of the Camino del Diablo versus the more heavily-traveled Gila Trail immediately to the north was the belief that they would not be subject to depredations by hostile "Apache."* Once on the Camino del Diablo, though, travelers not only suffered from the appalling heat and the interminable distances between reliable waterholes, but they were attacked, robbed, and murdered by the Sand Pápago as well as border bandits from Mexico. Childs, who was married to the daughter of one of the slayers, wrote: "The Pápago committed so many murders along Camino del Diablo that the Mexicans finally sent in the troops . . .

---

* *Apache* was a loose, often inaccurate term used by immigrants and settlers to describe Native Americans.

Bruce Lohman recovers as the Camino del Diablo stretches to the horizon.

while gathering them up, they killed quite a few of them." No Sand Pápago was more feared, or respected, by Mexican soldiers than Queléle, "carrion hawk." Arrested by Mexican troops and ordered shot, Queléle stared them down and said "I'm a Mexican buzzard. I eat dead Mexicans!" A Mexican officer let the Sand Pápago medicine man go, saying "Whoever talks to me like that deserves to live!"

However the family of eight died on the Devil's Road, theirs was not the most tragic milepost on the Camino del Diablo. The lives of many others were lost along the haunting stretch of the Camino del Diablo beyond; wrote Capt. Gaillard: "It was hard to imagine a more desolate or depressing ride. Mile after mile the journey stretches through this land of 'silence, solitude, and sunshine,' with little to distract the eye from the awful surrounding dreariness and desolation except bleaching skeletons of horses and the painfully frequent crosses which mark the graves of those who have perished of thirst."

It's not without irony that this section of the ancient Camino del Diablo is now a Border Patrol "drag road." A web of modern footpaths bisect the Camino del Diablo between the Circle-of-8 and Tinajas Altas, and trackers use the "lower drag" to cut sign of illegal immigrants. Few Mexican nationals, however, know of the life-saving tinajas that border their desperate paths as they march northward through the smoldering skeleton-littered borderlands in search of the new El Dorado.

Like so many others who struggled before us, our destination is also Tinajas Altas; the craggy white ridges of this desert sierra beckon us in the distance, as the wind-whipped sand continues to rake us. But our fallen companion is slow to recover, and the fierce sun continues to burn down on him. So Dave and I shade Bruce with our bodies and cover his head and neck with wet bandanas.

A Marine to the bone, Bruce struggles to his feet and marches stoically down the Devil's Road. Watching him gut-out the last few miles across the Lechuguilla Desert to Tinajas Altas, I'm reminded of the extraordinary ordeal of Pablo Valencia. In 1905, the forty-year old prospector struggled for six-and-a-half days without water in the brutal August heat to reach Tinajas Altas alive. On August 23, anthropologist W.J. McGee and a Pápago tracker named José were awakened at dawn by the terrible wail and rattling breath of Pablo; in *Desert Thirst as Disease*, McGee described the ghastly apparition of the man whose life he and José saved: "Pablo was stark naked; his formerly full-muscled legs and arms were shrunken and scrawny; his ribs ridged out like those of a starveling horse; his habitually plethoric abdomen was drawn in almost against his vertrebral column; his lips had disappeared as if amputated, leaving low edges of blackened tissue; his teeth and gums projected like those of a skinned animal, but the flesh was black and dry as a hank of beef jerky; his nose was withered and shrunken to half its length; the nostril-lining showing black; his eyes were set in a winkless stare, with surrounding skin so contracted as to expose the conjunctiva, itself black as the gums; his face was dark as a negro, and his skin generally turned a ghastly purplish yet ashen gray, with great livid blotches and streaks; his lower legs and feet, with forearms and hands, were torn and scratched by contact with thorns and sharp rocks, yet even the freshest cuts were as so many scratches in dry leather, without traces of blood or serum; his joints and bones stood out like those of a wasted sickling, though the

A desert bighorn sheep skull at a dry tinaja on the Camino del Diablo.

skin clung to them in a way suggesting shrunken rawhide used in re-
pairing a broken wheel. From inspection and handling, I estimated his
weight at 115 to 120 pounds. We soon found him deaf to all but loud
sounds, and so blind as to distinguish nothing save light and dark. The
mucous membrane lining his mouth and throat was shriveled, cracked,
and blackened, and his tongue shrunken to a mere bunch of black
integument. His respiration was slow, spasmodic, and accompanied by
a deep guttural moaning or roaring—the sound that awakened us a
quarter of a mile away. His extremities were cold as the surrounding
air; no pulsation could be detected in his wrists, and there was apparently little if any circulation beyond the knees and elbows; the heartbeat
was slow, irregular, fluttering, and almost ceasing . . . "

Long before Pablo Valencia's miraculous tale of survival, Raphael
Pumpelly wrote that immigrants struggling to reach Tinajas Altas had
to travel down a "long avenue between rows of mummified cattle,
horses, and sheep . . . This weird avenue had been made by some travelers with a sense of humor, and with a fertile imagination which had
not been deadened by thirst."

There is little humor remaining when we reach the foot of the Tinajas Altas Mountains at 11:30 AM. Joe McCraw, a legendary Border Patrol tracker who, with Dave, has saved scores of tough Mexicans like Pablo Valencia is there waiting for us. He helps us coax Bruce into a pictograph-covered cave at the foot of High Tanks.

Known to the Sand Pápago as *Óovak* (Where the Arrows Were Shot), Tinajas Altas was one of the principal encampments for this small indigenous group that was never believed to number more than several hundred people. While camped at the foot of this magnificent desert sierra in 1699, Padre Kino recounted one of the only eyewitness accounts of the Sand Pápago's desperate existence: "Here Manje counted thirty naked and poverty-stricken Indians who lived solely on roots, lizards, and other wild foods."

Through the years that followed the Sand Pápago's seasonal occupation of Óovak, desperate men and women struggled on their hands and knees to reach this ancient waterhole; a series of ten rock tanks that Camino del Diablo historian Bill Broyles estimates to hold 21,491 gallons of water when full, Tinajas Altas had enough water to slake anyone's thirst. But the lowest, most accessible pools were always the first to evaporate, and men reportedly wore their fingers to the bone trying to climb up the steep granite slabs to reach the "high tanks" of Tinajas Altas. In 1917 Kirk Bryan counted sixty-five graves on the *Mesita del Muerto* (Little Mesa of the Dead) below Tinajas Altas. But whether the death toll for this historic killing ground was four hundred people as the International Boundary Commission estimated in 1896, or two thousand people as Raphael Pumpelly wrote in 1915, one thing is certain: the Camino del Diablo's death toll was, as the International Boundary Commission first reported, "without parallel in North America."

Bruce remains passed out in the shade of the Mesita del Muerto while Dave and I scramble up the white granite slabs to the High Tanks of Tinajas Altas. The clatter of rock fall dislodged by desert bighorn sheep can be heard on the ridgetops above, as we dip our metal cups in the deep pool of water to fill our battered empty water jugs. I stare east through the v-slotted window of the canyon walls, and the sear white track of the Camino del Diablo severes the faint braid of immigrant trails

Historic grave. At one time, the Camino del Diablo was marked by the graves of 150 victims who died en route to the California goldfields during the 1850s and 1860s.

that cross the blistering no-man's land to the north. How many are suffering out there right now, wandering aimlessly in circles for the sweet taste of cool water that now slakes our parched thirst? How many will make it out of the desert alive so they can work in the underbelly of the American dream? How many will go down and give into the madness of thirst, unable to muster the incredible will of Pablo Valencia? How many more will leave little trace of their passing, but the flimsy plastic grocery bags that once held their worldly posessions: tortillas, chilis, salt, limes, canned sardines, beans, and goat cheese; an old flashlight, a wad of ancient pesos, and a matchbook etched with a ranch foreman's phone number; and finally, a black corpse.

It is 5:00 PM when the three of us trudge away from the cool shade and safety of Tinajas Altas; our stomachs are bloated with water, and we are carrying six gallons of water each for the forty-mile-long *jornada* (that part of a desert journey without water), through the Yuma Desert first pioneered by Spaniard Juan Bautista de Anza during an exploratory expedition in 1774. Looped together with bandanas *mojado*-style, we carry two gallons of water in each hand, and another two gallons in our packs. But at more than eight pounds a gallon, our loads are staggering, and it takes us four hours to thread the stony corridor of Smuggler's Pass through a breach in the Tinajas Altas Mountains. It is 9:00 PM when we reach our dry camp at BM 963, seven miles out on the barren sweep of the Davis Plain.

Our sheets and bedrolls provide little respite from the burning sand, and as weary as I am, I cannot sleep. The sand is baking moisture out of my body, and I'm forced to drink water throughout the night. We have thirty-two miles of blistering desert to cross before we can come in out of this smothering heat, and as the white stars track across the black heavens I start to count down, frequently lifting the wet bandana from my sunburned eyelids to peer at the luminescent green hands of my watch as they crawl in circles on my wrist. But I can't wait any longer. By 4:00 AM, I'm boiling old coffee grounds which Dave says "smell like pipe tobacco." And by 4:50 AM we are moving. My legs are swollen with edema and blistered with heat rash, but fortunately we've each hit our stride. We march through the dawn shadows of the Tinajas Altas Mountains as they give way to the receding shadowline of the 3,171-foot Gila Mountains. At noon, we lay up near the crossroads of yet another deadly immigrant route which crosses the craggy flanks of the Gila Mountains through Dripping Springs Canyon. By 5:00 PM we are walking again: three miles an hour, an hour on, ten minutes off, the same relentless pace we've tried to maintain since leaving Ajo six days ago. But ten miles short of our goal, we run out of water—one by one. Fortunately, we enter the killing zone at nightfall, and nothing can stop us now except sunrise. Or a sidewinder.

In the distance the lights of the Yuma foothills float slowly toward us through the dark muggy night, but as hard as we chase them, they never seem to get any closer . . . until suddenly we find ourselves in the middle of a ghost town, surrounded by vacant trailers, empty pads, and houses abandoned by Yuma's winter snowbirds. We look around, but no one's home; they're holed up in Minnesota, Oregon, Saskatchewan, and elsewhere until this deadly six-month heat wave passes. Fifty miles southeast of here, hundreds of Mexican citizens have had a similar bizarre experience: they've marched for thirty or forty miles through the burning heat, snakes, cactus, rocks, and scorpions toward a mirage of buildings drifting on the horizonline, while dreaming of family, food, but especially water—only to discover they'd stumbled into a ghost town of olive drab buildings used as targets for military operations on the Barry M. Goldwater Range. Their hopes dashed, they stumble down the dusty streets with empty water jugs and little promise of crossing the tortured ground beyond to Interstate 8.

We are more fortunate. It is 9:30 PM when we finally stagger down the pavement to Bruce's house on El Camino del Diablo Drive. The beer's in the fridge, he doesn't have the keys, and nobody's home. But at least the Road of the Devil is finally at our backs. The same cannot be said for the others who are still out there, right now; they are struggling toward the American dream, but they face the death mask of Pablo Valencia, a half-filled jug of urine pressed to their cracked lips, a black corpse swinging in the hot wind, or the hovering shadows of Mexican buzzards still screaming the words of Queléle.

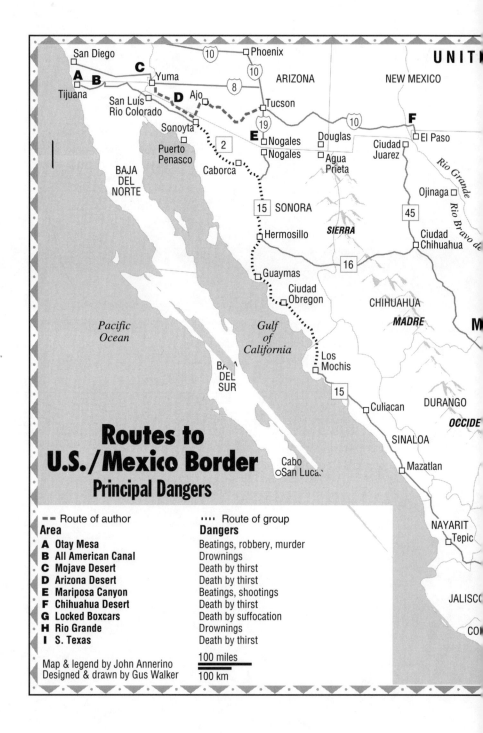

San Diego

Phoenix

UNITE

C

A **B** Yuma

Tijuana

D Ajo

San Luis
Rio Colorado

ARIZONA

NEW MEXICO

10

10

8

Tucson

Sonoyta

19

10

F

E

Nogales

Douglas

El Paso

2

Nogales

Ciudad
Juarez

Puerto
Penasco

Caborca

Agua
Prieta

Rio Grande

BAJA
DEL
NORTE

Ojinaga

Rio Bravo de

15

SONORA

45

Hermosillo

SIERRA

Ciudad
Chihuahua

16

Guaymas

Ciudad
Obregon

CHIHUAHUA

*Pacific
Ocean*

*Gulf
of
California*

MADRE

M

Los
Mochis

BA ^
DEL
SUR

15

Culiacan

DURANGO

OCCIDE

Routes to
U.S./Mexico Border

SINALOA

Cabo
San Luca.

Mazatlan

Principal Dangers

NAYARIT

Tepic

JALISCO

CO

COi

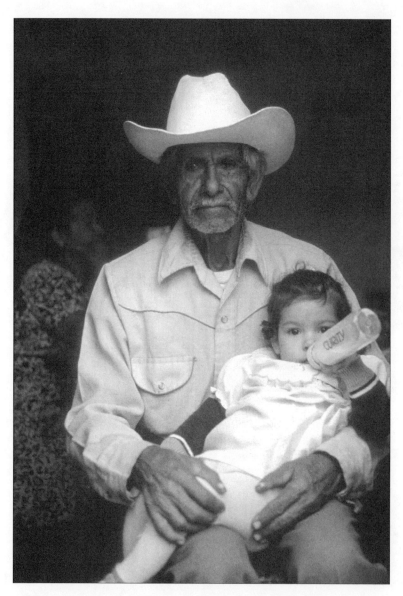

El Viejo. After a long day of toiling in the fields of Las Gallinas, Sinaloa,
Marcelino Ruíz senior holds his granddaughter Diana while his son Rosario
tries to cross the U.S./Mexico border.

† 2 †

OLD MEXICO

†

"Dear and beautiful Mexico
when I die far from you,
they'll tell you I'm sleeping
and bring me back to you."

Jorge Negrete
México Lindo

WHEN I FIRST see El Viejo, the old campesino is sitting on a feeble wooden chair. He is worn out after a long day of working in the fields, and he is clutching his granddaughter in his gnarled, calloused hands. His dark eyes are pools of sorrow. His craggy face is etched with deep lines that trace back to his boyhood in the sierra. And his brittle bones are weary from carrying the burdens and dreams of his family. But the young girl cradled in his arms beams with love and warmth that will force him to work stooped-over until the day he dies. Or until *Tata Dios* Himself provides a better way.

I am sitting outside his small house in Las Gallinas, Sinaloa when El Viejo's story spills out. Chickens are pecking at the dirt beneath the pink bougainvillea, pigs are squealing in a nearby pen, and a diesel-fueled truck rumbles down the highway when I start taking down his tale.

His name is Marcelino Ruíz, and for as far back as he can remember, the bloodlines of his people have mixed with the Mayo, the Tarahumara, the half-Indian Mestizos. And for nearly as long, they have followed the verdant course of the Río Fuerte from the lofty heights of the Sierra Madre Occidental, through the sub-tropical thorn forests

33

that guard its rugged foothills, into the lush river valleys and farmlands of Sinaloa. From sunup till sunset, they work as peons, tilling fields that will never be theirs, for wages that never stave off hunger.

Porfiria Castro-Váldez' story was not much different. Born in the foothills of the Sierra Madre in La Villa de Choix in 1923, her day also begins at first light. That's when she collects eggs from her white hens, pats out corn tortillas in her firm hands, and brews sweet *café con leche* that sustains her husband Marcelino throughout his long hard day.

In the dirt-poor pueblito of Las Gallinas, their first child was born. The brown-eyed baby brought them happiness and hope, but as he grew older he brought them sadness and despair when tortillas, beans, and atole didn't always fill their gaunt stomachs. One day of back-breaking work stretched into the next, but the Ruíz family stood together with love, tradition, and devotion to the Virgen de Guadalupe.

Two decades later, their son Rosario came of age and married a girl from the village nearby. Her name is Guadalupe López-Ruíz and together with Rosario she had three beautiful children. They named them Joel, Diana, and Sonia. As tradition dictated, Rosario's young family continued to live under the same thatched roof with his aging parents. But that's when Rosario's path to work extended beyond the lush green fields surrounding Las Gallinas, when he first realized the wages of a campesino could no longer feed his entire family.

No one in Las Gallinas I spoke with is exactly sure when the new trail was followed north from the rich fields of cotton, sugar cane, and mango orchards of Sinaloa into the grim deserts of America's borderlands. But the seasonal exodus began not long after the Bracero Work Program ended in 1964. Men returning from the camps in California and Arizona talked of a trail through the desert; it was long, hot, and dangerous, but being tough Sinaloenses who worked like dogs for the rich gringos, they could cross it to avoid La Migra. And many did, though they still speak in hushed reverence of those who could not.

For over three decades, men from Las Gallinas have left their families and followed the deadly trail and tales of riches north to the new El Dorado. And for three generations they have sent their money home. Their modest dreams were to buy their own plot of land, build a small adobe for their family, raise chickens, goats, and pigs, and grow a *mil-pita* of corn, tomatoes, chilis, and manzanilla. At the very least, they needed to feed their families.

El Viejo was not one of them. He tells me he never had the desire to leave his family to work in the north, but his son Rosario was different. Perhaps it was the divine intervention of Tata Dios, he couldn't say. But Rosario's cousin Marcelino Ruíz also wanted to go north; he lived in a one-room dwelling with his wife, three children, and his mother-in-law. Their friends Armando Ortega and Guillermo Torres also wanted to go. Armando, still unmarried, lived in a *casa de cartón* (cardboard shack) with a family of six. Guillermo lived nearby in a spartan room with his pregnant wife and their young son Guillermo Jr. But each of them had recently been caught by La Migra while trying to cross the border; they signed voluntary departure forms and returned to Las Gallinas. Without work, none of them had the option of staying behind and waiting for money to fall out of the sky. Rosario and Marcelino had more mouths to feed than Armando and Guillermo; just as importantly, they had the ability to pay for another ten-hour bus trip north to the frontier. But by the time I received Rosario's letter inviting me to Las Gallinas, he and Marcelino had already boarded another crowded, second class bus for the 500-mile run to the border. Neither Rosario or Marcelino wanted their wives to worry; so they didn't tell them where they were going, how they would slip across the border, or if they had to stare death in the face again by trying to cross the killing desert. Nor would the women know where their husbands went until they received a call on the village phone telling them that money was being wired to them, or that their husband had vanished in the desert.

Like most of the women in Las Gallinas, Sinaloa, Tlaticuapán, Jalisco, and who really knew how many other poverty-stricken campos, pueblos, and colonial cities throughout the Republic of Mexico, Rosario's and Marcelino's wives only knew the loneliness of their husband's absence. They didn't know the dangers of their journey. You could see the hope, longing, and despair in their eyes, as they struggled from day to day— making tortillas, sorting out beans, and washing clothes by hand in a 50-gallon water drum that once held toxic insecticide; these were the

El Viejo's wife Porfiría Castro-Valdéz tends to the daily chore of rolling out corn tortillas with an empty bottle, while her grandchild Sonia looks on.

small rituals which marked their days and nights as they held their families together.

Of Mexico's estimated forty million poor who live in poverty-racked colonias—including the estimated one million indigenous people who've been forcefully displaced from their homelands by land fraud, drug cultivation, environmental devastation, and an exploding mestizo population—most dream of a better life than can be had on national wages that now equal .35¢ an hour or 200 pesos every *quincena* (semi-monthly pay period). For many, there is no choice: cross the desert borderlands or starve.

When I visited Armando outside the cardboard shanty he shared with a family of six, he proudly wore a pair of American Levis as pigs rooted up the barren hillside around us; he said he was trying to earn enough money to make another crossing. So was Guillermo, who hoped one day to move his pregnant wife and young son out of their one-room dwelling into their own modest adobe. At peon's wages, it could take two or three months to save enough money for another border crossing. But

Otomí Indians
Raymunda Feliciano
and her two sons beg
for tokens of mercy
in the streets of
Guanajuato, Mexico
after being forcefully
displaced from their
traditional homelands;
they are part of an
estimated 1 million
indigenous people in
Mexico who've been
driven from their
ancestral lands.

there was little work to be had in the fields nearby, they told me. And neither Armando or Guillermo were sure where Rosario and Marcelino would try crossing the border again. It was probably the desert, but they were either going to Arizona or to Florida to work in the citrus groves; so it could be anywhere along the 1,952-mile long U.S./Mexico border that stretched from the Pacific Ocean to the Gulf of Mexico.

Rosario and Marcelino could have gone to Baja California Norte and tried crossing the border near Tijuana into California, but it is a risky, expensive, and dangerous place to cross. (Of more than 1.4 million illegal immigrants apprehended during the first eleven months of 1998, 232,827 were caught near San Diego.) Once caught, a person needed money to live on the border while he tried again and again to elude the border sensors, posses of Border Patrol agents aided with dogs, horses, jeeps, night vision scopes, thermal imaging, and helicopters wielding FLIR (Forward Looking Infrared) night vision and blinding Night Sun spotlights; or he had to pay a *coyote* the equivalent of a month's wages in a Los Angeles sweat shop to take him across. Those Mexicans citizens and Central Americans who weren't caught by La Migra or shaken down by Mexican police faced the prospect of drowning in the Tijuana River, dying from a fall off a cliff, getting in a wreck trying to outrun the Border Patrol, or being beaten, robbed, raped, or murdered by their own countrymen who stalked them in the dark haunts of places like Deadman Canyon and Otay Mesa in south San Diego.

An illegal immigrant could try crossing the sand dunes east of Mexicali, and if he didn't die of thirst, he might very well drown in the deep, swift-moving, slick-walled All American Canal even before trying to cross the Mojave Desert beyond.* Some public works employees have called the grisly, bloated bodies of drowning victims "floaters."

He could try the canyons of Nogales, Arizona, but if he wasn't beaten or shot by the Mexican police, an Arizona rancher, or a rogue Border Patrol agent, he still had to cross a dangerous drug corridor in order to pay a coyote one hundred dollars or more for the taxi ride north to Tucson or Phoenix.

He could try swimming the Río Grande; known in Mexico as the Río Bravo del Norte, the thousand-mile stretch of the benign-looking river forms the eastern half of the U.S./Mexico border and claims the lives of many Mexican immigrants each year.**

Or he could ride the rails and risk suffocating in a locked Texas boxcar, or try crossing the searing south Texas brushlands north of Laredo.†

Rosario, Marcelino, Armando, and Guillermo could try a hundred

---

* In July, 1998, seven Mexican nationals died of thirst after being abandoned by their *coyote* in the Mojave Desert near Salton City, California. The mummified corpse of another victim was later found three miles away. And hikers reported seeing two other corpses that had not been relocated by authorities.

** According to a University of Houston study, "Death at the Border," 1,185 people died trying to cross the U.S./Mexico border between 1993-1996; 72%, or 851 people, drowned while trying to cross canals or the Río Grande.

† Fifty-three people died of thirst in 1998 while crossing the Texas borderlands.

other ways to cross the border. There were many roads that led to it, to death, or to the American dream.

Or they could take the easy way out. Many had. And few would blame them. They could ride a bus 150 miles south to Culiacán, Sinaloa, the drug crossroads and murder capitol of Mexico, make a *manda* (religious promise) to *narcosantón* Jesús Malverde, the patron saint of Mexican drug dealers, and become cocaine cowboys. With Mexico's Bolsa Nacional repeatedly gutted by the devaluation of the peso, corrupt politicians, and a ruling elite which continues to funnel the future of its citizens into secret bank accounts that stretch from Houston and the Cayman Islands to Switzerland, and fails to provide an economic infrastructure and the most basic necessities for its poverty-stricken citizens—the temptations of an economy now fueled by fifteen to thirty billion dollars a year in narcodollars are all around the Las Gallinas of Mexico. How easy it would be to trade in leather huaraches for the snug fit of white lizardskin boots; their sweat-stained bandanas for heavy gold chains they could hand out like candy to the almond-eyed young *chicas* in Los Mochis and on the beaches of Mazatlán; their tired old bicycles for 4x4 pickups, customized with rows of K.C. lights, chrome wheels, stolen Arizona or California plates, and stereos blaring the latest narco corridos; their wooden-handled machetes for snakeskin bandoliers carrying the weapons of Mexico's latest revolution: a beeper, cellular, speed-loader clips of teflon-coated slugs, a bone-handled .45 semi-automatic, and *Cuernos de Chivo* (AK-47) with a fifty-round drum for when things get heavy. It could be so easy, and the cumbersome duffle bags of American cash they'd have to smuggle back across border into Old Mexico—the equivalent of 2.5 kilos of hundred dollar bills for every kilo of cocaine—would help so many people in Las Gallinas. The new "picudos" could build schools, clinics, and churches, and the women, children, and weary campesinos would sing *narco corridos* (folk songs of drug traffickers) to these modern-day Mexican Robin Hoods, as they have done since the 1940s.

> "Gone is Pablito, friend of the poor,
> Killed by the government

In a world that shows no mercy
For people like that.
And the gringos, laughing on the other side
of the river,
Prayed for Pablito to die.
Yet he had done nothing more
Than give them what they wanted."*

But Rosario and Marcelino, like Armando and Guillermo and most of the illegal immigrants Americans still depend on to do the work no one else will do, chose not to enter *La Vida* (The Life)—or even to carry a backpack of marijuana across the border for a few hundred dollars as a onetime shot through the canyons of Nogales, Arizona. Neither saints nor desperados, they chose not to become part of the estimated ten percent of illegal immigrants who crowd American prisons and cost taxpayers twenty-two thousand dollars a head each year. They chose hard work instead. An honest day's wages for an honest day of stoop labor in the broiling sun.

Only, they had to survive a killing ground to get jobs even panhandling gringos seemed to shun.

In the case of Rosario and Marcelino, that probably means trying to cross the desert again, because they figure it is safer and cheaper, and that there is less risk of being caught by La Migra. Besides, that's where the men from Las Gallinas nearly always crossed—in spite of the tragic deaths that periodically devastated their heroic odysseys.

Yet, each year they go, convinced they can walk forty, sixty, one hundred miles or more across the deadliest desert in North America. But they do not even have the means of carrying their precious cargo of water on burros and mules, as so many of their country-men had when they perished en masse on the Camino del Diablo, trying to reach the California goldfields during the 1850s and 1860s. Nor do they possess the luxuries gringo backpackers use for leisurely weekend outings. The poor, tough men from Las Gallinas will be wearing cheap rubber shower san-

---

* *Drug Lord: The Life and Death of a Mexican Kingpin*, pg. 264, by Terrence E. Poppa. New York: Pharos Books,1990.

The future of Mexico. The women and children who were left behind, while Rosario and his cousin Marcelino looked for work in the United States. As I made this picture, my taxi driver whispered: *"Ese es el futuro de México— mujeres y niños."* (That's the future of Mexico—women and children.)

dals and ill-fitting baseball cleats to protect their feet from the rocks, thorns, hot sand, and lava, not form-fitting one hundred dollar hiking boots; they will carry their meager rations of tortillas, beans, sardines, and chilis in flimsy white plastic bags, not freeze-dried gourmet meals cooked over shiny white gas stoves carried in expensive goretex backpacks. And they will sleep on the scorched bare earth in thin cotton t-shirts, not in cozy two hundred dollar, down sleeping bags. They will follow vague routes, passed down from one desperate generation to the next, across a horizonless no-man's land, not well-manicured trails. Their signposts will be sun-bleached bones, empty plastic water jugs, a distant mountain, not hand-painted fluorescent signs with arrows pointing the trail every quarter-mile. They will cross a merciless desert for jobs, not for scenic vistas. And they will try crossing it during the deadly summer months when harvest work is most plentiful, not during the clear, brisk days of a glorious Sonoran Desert winter when bird watchers delight in counting colorful migrating birds that flit from one cactus blossom to another. And nothing will stop these honest people in their quest for a better life, not the killing desert, and not the transformation of the "tortilla curtain" into the Iron Curtain.

With Armando and Guillermo close behind, Rosario and Marcelino have left a campo stricken with loneliness and despair, filled with woman, children, and old men too old to face the grueling journey or who, like El Viejo, simply never wanted to go.

I say my farewells, and take a long hard look at Guadalupe, Porfiría, and Marcelino's wife. They are clinging to the warmth and love of their children, and they don't have a clue their brave husbands have embarked upon the corridor of death during the killing season to feed them.

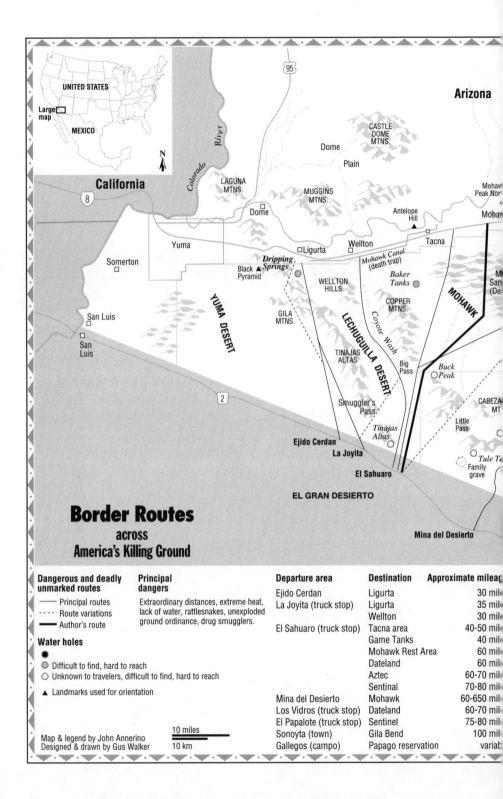

Border Routes
across
America's Killing Ground

Dangerous and deadly unmarked routes
— Principal routes
--- Route variations
▬ Author's route

Water holes
●
◐ Difficult to find, hard to reach
○ Unknown to travelers, difficult to find, hard to reach

▲ Landmarks used for orientation

Principal dangers
Extraordinary distances, extreme heat, lack of water, rattlesnakes, unexploded ground ordinance, drug smugglers.

Map & legend by John Annerino
Designed & drawn by Gus Walker

10 miles
10 km

Departure area	Destination	Approximate mileage
Ejido Cerdan	Ligurta	30 mil
La Joyita (truck stop)	Ligurta	35 mil
	Wellton	30 mil
El Sahuaro (truck stop)	Tacna area	40-50 mil
	Game Tanks	40 mil
	Mohawk Rest Area	60 mil
	Dateland	60 mil
	Aztec	60-70 mil
	Sentinal	70-80 mil
Mina del Desierto	Mohawk	60-650 mil
Los Vidros (truck stop)	Dateland	60-70 mil
El Papalote (truck stop)	Sentinel	75-80 mil
Sonoyta (town)	Gila Bend	100 mil
Gallegos (campo)	Papago reservation	variab

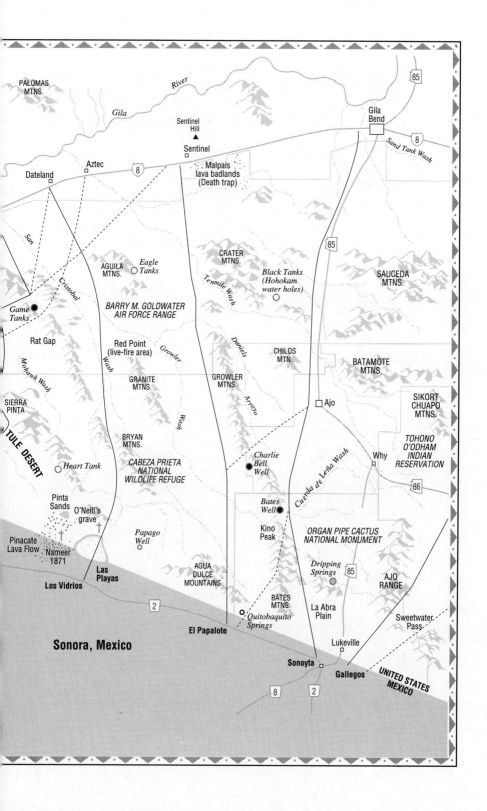

El Sahuaro. Rosario (front) and Marcelino stride beneath the landmark saquaro cactus that stood sentinel at the gateway to the hell we had entered.

† 3 †

PATH OF FIRE

†

"Seventeen miles from the border, I saw a body face down
in the sand, completely dressed in pants and shirt. This body
appeared to have been there for ten days, as there were some
dry blood spots around it."

Carlos Cobarubia Mesa,
upon crossing the desert of *El Sahuaro*

I T IS AFTER MIDNIGHT. The heat is still smothering me. And I
am lying on the scorched, bare earth next to four strange men who,
others warned me, "will slit your throat for your water." Just how
soon they will sever my jugular and leave me choking on warm blood
in the hot sand is not certain. But it will only be a matter of hours—
maybe twelve, no more than eighteen—before we run out of water, and
I'm forced to come to grips with that warning.

It is August 20, and there is no escaping this droning, deadly heat
which patiently waits to suck the very marrow from our bones. We are lying
in the same open grave Carlos Cobarubia Mesa struggled across a year earlier; that's when he stared down in horror at the first of three corpses he
stumbled across during his daring seventy-mile trek across the American
desert. Stretched out in the hot sand next to me, still dressed in long pants
and shirts, are four men who are betting their lives they can do what
would kill most trained athletes and hardened desert rats: that, like Carlos Cobarubia Mesa, they too can march fifty, seventy, one hundred miles
or more across the deadliest desert in North America in hopes of finding
tough, poor-paying jobs most Americans wouldn't consider taking.

Midnight camp. Marcelino takes first watch for *La Migra*, while (left to right) Rosario, Armando, and Guillermo try to sleep in the hot sand at our bivouac in Big Pass at the foot of the Buck Mountains.

With nothing more than a thin cotton shirt to insulate my body from the burning salt pan, I stare up at the fiery heavens and realize that the odds of any of us making it out of this desert alive are staggering. And now it would only be a matter of hours before fate showed me the hand we'd been dealt: these men would either be caught by Border Patrol trackers, and I would photograph their apprehension; we would all die like dogs in a killing ground that has claimed hundreds—perhaps thousands—of their countrymen; or maybe, just maybe, we would actually reach that burning, black river of asphalt called Interstate 8.

At best, I now realized, that was little more than a hallucination. It is 4:45 AM, and a white light burns over the eastern horizon. It ignites our camp in Big Pass between the 2,629-foot Buck Mountains and the 2,888-foot Copper Mountains, a dozen miles north of the Camino del Diablo, and it enshrouds this grim landscape with a hair-singeing heat that will continue torching the Lechuguilla Desert for another two months.

This tract of no-man's land forms what some naturalists consider to be the heart of the Sonoran Desert, a one hundred six thousand square

The Barry M. Goldwater Range is one of the last refuges for the endangered Sonoran pronghorn antelope.

mile region that extends across the length of the eight hundred mile long Baja Peninsula, half of the Mexican state of Sonora, part of southeastern California, and most of southwestern Arizona. Lowest and hottest among North America's five great deserts, including the Mojave, Great Basin, Chihuahuan, and Painted Deserts, the Sonoran Desert ranges in elevation from sea level on the shores of the Sea of Cortés to five thousand feet in the mountains of Arizona; it has a rainfall pattern that varies from less than four inches to more than eighteen inches of precipitation a year. Arguably lush, and estimated to be ten thousand years old, the Sonoran Desert hosts a rich bio-diversity of plant and animal life considered unmatched in the deserts that border it and the natural life zones, or biomes, that thrive above it. Home to the endangered Sonoran pronghorn antelope, the majestic desert bighorn sheep, and the coyote, bird life includes road runners, Gambel's quail, white wing dove, and golden eagles, and among its reptiles the chuckwalla, Gila monster, and Mexican beaded lizard, as well as the tortoise and diamondback rattlesnake. Plants range from spectacular forests of saguaro cactus to burned-out creosote flats. Environmentalists envision such country as being protected in the coming millennium as the Sonoran Desert National Park, when the military's lease expires on the Barry M. Goldwater Range. But what is the field laboratory of the occasional scientist and the playground of hunters and naturalists the six fairest months of the year remains the merciless haunt of illegal immigrants and Border Patrol trackers the six most brutal months of the year.

"*¿Listos?*" (Ready?) Rosario asks. We stare at each other silently, fearing what lies beyond in the empty maw of the Mohawk Desert and the lethal sand trap of its namesake dunes. *"Andele, pués,"* (Let's go, then.) Rosario urges us. We struggle to our feet and resume our march north into oblivion, clinging to the belief that we will reach the Interstate alive.

Months earlier, I had run 750 miles of Arizona wilderness from Mexico to Utah, in part as a way of exploring the ancient ways of Native American routes and running. And, having crossed that hard country, I was now having serious doubts about crossing this particular point of no return. We are little more than twenty miles north of Mexico's Highway 2 in a region criss-crossed by *narcotraficantes*, and we have thirty to fifty miles or more to go—depending on our angle of travel— before this modern *despoblado* is at our backs. But we are already down to 1½ gallons of water each, and it's simply not enough to reach the distant horizon and the illusory promise of life which awaits each of us on the other side of Interstate 8. The perspiration evaporates immediately on our hot brown skin, forming an itchy crust of salt that must be constantly scraped away in long red streaks: evidence that we will run out of water much sooner than we'd anticipated. But a man I had never met before has prepared me for just such an emergency. Bill Broyles, a seasoned desert explorer and historian, has provided me with the one insurance policy that will save our lives if everything goes to hell. I hope. On my map, he's carefully plotted the locations of ancient Sand Pápago *tinajas* which have remained hidden from generations of Mexican immigrants who struggled and died within the long shadows of the rugged desert sierras that still hide those precious waterholes. And I'm betting my life on that information, and my gut feeling that this man can be trusted implicitly.

I tell Rosario my concerns, then ask him: "*¿Necesitamos agua? Allá*

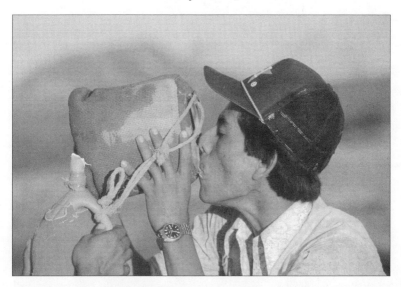

Rosario takes a long drink from a burlap-covered water jug.

hay." (Do we need water? It's there.) I point to a steep dark canyon fun-
neling out of the Buck Mountains.

It empties its detritous into an alluvial *bajada*, "lowland," that fans
out across the stark Lechuguilla Desert.

"No, es okay. No necesitamos. Andele, pués." (No, it's okay. We don't
need any. Let's go.) Rosario marches on, leading his cousin Marcelino
and their two friends Armando and Guillermo across the trailless
desert, guided only by the distant landmark of Mohawk Peak North—
and he is maintaining the same relentless four-mile-an-hour pace he held
throughout the hot black night before. I run after them, the cameras and
water jugs bouncing on my sweat-soaked t-shirt, and I think to myself
maybe there is a chance we can make it to the Interstate if we hold this
pace till 11:00 AM, lay up in the shade out of the noonday sun, and break
for the blacktop under the cover and coolness of darkness.

But that notion is dispelled two hours later. That's when we reach
the Mohawk Drag, our fourth Border Patrol drag road thus far. Rosario
tells me we must hide until La Migra goes by. Then we can tiptoe across
the drag road, and my companions will carefully brush out our tracks with

Brushing Out.
Using the branches
of a creosote bush,
Armando brushes out
our tracks on a Border
Patrol "drag road"
in hopes of eluding
La Migra.

branches ripped from a creosote bush. Just weeks earlier, I'd photographed Border Patrol trackers Joe McCraw and Dave Roberson at
work in what they called the Tacna corridor; so I know they have already
cruised or flown this sandy drag road at sunup, or they'll wait for the long
shadows of sundown to "cut sign." Either way, I've been with them both
when they tracked men down by detecting their faint "brushouts." So
I know we should keep moving before the heat lays down on us for
good. But I am not this group's *coyote*; I am a photojournalist, driven by
a lifelong promise to document the struggle of illegal immigrants across
America's killing ground, not to "aid and abet." And as at odds as I am
with their dangerous decision to wait—having devoted a decade of my
life teaching wilderness survival, and how to avoid just such perils—I
have little choice but to wait with my companions in this carnivorous

La Migra. The image of La Migra lurked in the group's thoughts and actions.

heat, as it continues to chew away at our chances of escaping from the desert alive.

But I tell myself I will not let it come to dying: if someone goes down, I will use my signal mirror to flash a Marine fighter pilot screaming across the R-2301 west half of the Barry M. Goldwater Range. Failing that, if my mirror flashes are mistaken for one of the hundreds of aluminum tow darts imbedded in the floor of this bombing range like huge silver arrowheads, I will wait until nightfall, leave my cameras behind, and make a last ditch run to Interstate 8 and call in the Marines' helicopter-borne Rescue-1. But I will not sit idly by and watch any of these men die, I promise myself that.

> "Twelve to thirteen miles from the first body, I saw another body. This body was wrapped in a white sheet. I did not go near it, so I cannot tell how long it had been there."
>
> Carlos Cobarubia Mesa

Sitting there miles from nowhere in the burning white sand, making promises I don't know if I can physically endure, I am suddenly struck by the heroic journey these four men have embarked upon. They have fled the dirt-poor campo of Las Gallinas, Sinaloa in hopes, like most American immigrants, of providing a better life for their families. They've criss-crossed dangerous smuggling routes on both sides of the line, now used by drug cartels who've moved their staging areas to the remote airstrips etched into the frontier of Sonora. They are braving the fearsome heat of the Camino del Diablo, the intensity of which was unknown in their own country in the foothills of the Sierra Madre. And they are knowingly walking across a "hot," or active gunnery range strafed and bombed regularly by F-15s, F-16s, A-10s, Harrier IIs, and littered with unexploded rockets, bombs, and 155mm Howitzer rounds. But their greatest fear, other than La Migra, are *las viboras* (the rattlesnakes). Throughout the long hours I wait with them for the phantom trackers

Military ordnance like this rocket were a constant reminder of the other hazards illegal immigrants face, in addition to extreme temperatures and poisonous snakes and scorpions, while crossing the Barry M. Goldwater Range, a bombing range.

to prowl past, they talk about both with the same contempt. I just listen. I don't tell them it's too hot for the deadly, cold-blooded pit vipers. Nor do I try explaining that Border Patrol trackers in this remote sector, like Roberson and McCraw, have saved over two hundred people who otherwise wouldn't have made it out of this desert alive.

Staring up through the branches of a creosote bush at the hot white sky, I suddenly realize I've formed strong bonds with men on both sides of the line: the men I've pitched myself into this life-and-death struggle with, and the men who are no doubt hunting us. These are sympathies I keep to myself, as I lie in the burning sand struggling with the irony that these people are risking their lives to cross the ancestral lands of the Sand Pápago, what—before the Gadsden Purchase of 1854—was considered their country. Then, I don't need to tell them what they already know: If this were Mexico, there would be a *pueblito* (little town),

Armando (left) slices goat cheese while his tired companions wait
for their rations.

rancho (ranch), or *pozo* (well), something, every ten or fifteen miles that
would make sense out of the endless sweep of burned-out creosote flats
which drift to the horizon in every direction. But here, there is nothing. Desert bighorn sheep and Sonoran pronghorn antelope are not to
be seen. Birds aren't heard singing in this claustrophobic heat. Life-giv-
ing water is nowhere near. Even the lizards have fled this hole on the
map. Yet generations of men have beaten well worn-paths across this *despoblado* and made it out alive. But the ground all around us is littered
with the remains of those who didn't make it—who died horribly from
thirst, or simply went mad from the emptiness.

No, my throat will not be slit by these men. I know that without a
doubt now; I was betting on it all along. But when I see the closest
thing they have to a knife is the file from the toenail clipper Armando
is trying to slice the goat cheese with, I start laughing. They're puzzled.
So I pull out my knife, point to our dwindling water supply, and draw
the back of the steel blade across my throat from one ear to the other.
Rosario points north and asks who told me such a thing, "*¿Los pinches*

gringos?" (The fucking gringos?) I nod. He shakes his head. We all laugh. I hand my open knife to Armando and he uses it to cut the salty white cheese they share with me, along with canned *frijoles* (pinto beans), corn tortillas, and chilis. If we die today, we will die together, struggling toward an Interstate choked with Americans fleeing this same oppressive heat on the crowded sands of San Diego.

Sated by the small meal, and our one stab at laughter, we try fleeing that same brain-addling heat, but it comes down on us like a billowing cloud of exhaust. And each time I breathe in and out, now, the hot air singes my parched throat, cracked lips, and blood-caked nostrils, "hih-hun, hih-huh, hih-huh . . . "

In hoarse voices, the men whisper faintly of home, their wives, their children, as their footsteps crunch northward through the burning wastes. For a moment, their talk bridges the emotional bonds I tried to discard before I descended into this inferno and, through the shimmering waves of heat refracting off the desert floor, I see her long black hair, I smell the musky scent of perfume and sweat, I see rivulets of hot red candle wax pooling around her mother's shrine to the Virgen de Guadalupe, I hear the sound of cúmbia music and the laughter of children playing beneath the street lamp on a hot summer night. But I can't dwell on such memories, or I'll come apart. I march on, licking my cracked lips with a scaly tongue. The heat is going to win now. I know. Only the shrill, throbbing whine of cicadas breaks the suffocating embrace of this sulphur white heat. Guillermo falls further and further behind. Rosario, Armando, and Marcelino plod on. But it will only be a matter of time before each of us is taken by the desert.

This ordeal began three days ago. That's when I left Tucson, Arizona a hundred fifty miles east of here, unsure of exactly what I was getting into. Apart from the obvious hazards of documenting the torturous summer trek of strangers in a desert bombing range that seldom showed any mercy between May and mid-September, I was faced with the logistical dilemma of how and where to link up with a group of illegal immigrants to cross the vast borderlands between Mexico's Highway 2 and U.S. Interstate 8, and where to leave my shuttle vehicle. Since the Border Patrol's nearest stations were located in Yuma and Tacna, forty miles east, I dropped my truck off in Gila Bend, which lies another seventy miles east of Tacna on Interstate 8. For all practical purposes, Interstate 8 was the finish line for immigrants lucky enough to emerge from a desert which, depending on their departure point and angle of travel, stretched thirty-five to 120 miles south to Mexico's Highway 2. Assuming I succeeded in linking up with a group, I further reasoned they would still be trying to elude trackers if we managed to escape from the desert; thus, wherever we hit the Interstate between Tacna and Gila Bend I figured I could hitchhike east to my truck.

Deciding where to leave my pickup was the easy part. Trying to find a group to cross the desert with in a virtually uninhabited region was going to be far more difficult, I realized, as a confidant drove me down Mexico's Highway 2 across a bleak expanse of empty ground that paralleled the international border.

Unpaved until 1955, this narrow strip of asphalt was once a rugged dirt track called the Albelardo L. Rodríguez Military Highway. Linkng mainland Mexico with the Baja Peninsula, Highway 2 still shadows the route of forty-niners who struggled and died en route to the California goldfields over a century earlier. Today, however, Highway 2 has become the starting line for immigrants crisscrossing the grim reaches of the Camino del Diablo immediately to north. Yet, along this stretch of Sonora's border with Arizona, Highway 2 was more than 140 miles across. From a logistical standpoint, it lacked a principal staging area like Tijuana's Colonia Libertad, where hundreds of immigrants gather each day before making their midnight bids to cross the border. So several weeks earlier, I had reconned the string of outposts and truckstops immigrants were most likely to use as departure points along this desolate stretch of U.S./Mexico border.

I first considered using the bustling bordertown of Sonoyta, Sonora as a crossing point, as thirty-one Salvadorans had done in 1980, before thirteen of them wandered to their deaths in Organ Pipe Cactus National Monument barely twenty miles north. But I eliminated it for two reasons: Even with a training regimen of running seventy miles a week for

Riddled by heavy arms and canon fire, a burned out pickup truck and boulder lie at the end of a remote airstrip used by drug smugglers south of El Sahuaro.

months on end during the heat of day as preperation for this trek, the odds of crossing the hundred miles of desert that stood between Sonoyta and Gila Bend with a group of strangers and all of us making it out alive were slim. Secondly, Sonoyta and its perimeters were patrolled by a nervous dragnet of machine gun-toting, teenage *Federales*; uniformed PJE (*Policia Judicial Estatal*), dressed in black ball caps, black sunglasses, black t-shirts, and packing trademark .45 semi-automatics; and heavily armed, plainclothes PJF (*Policia Judicial Federal*), who took their cue from B. Traven: "Badges . . . we don't need no stinking badges."

I also considered, but eliminated, the possibility of using the truck stop of Los Vidrios eighty kilometers west of Sonoyta as a departure point for many reasons: It was reportedly used less frequently as a crossing point than Highway 2's other principal truckstops like El Sahuaro and La Joyita. More importantly, though, was a recent phone tip I received in Tucson indicating that ownership of the once popular restauraunt had changed hands, and that Los Vidrios was being used by drug lords as a stash house; so I couldn't exactly hang around and listen to *narco corridos* the two or three days it might take me to connect with a group without drawing suspicions or the flesh-burning probes of a *chicharra* (cattle prod).

"Eres la flor más bonita
que está sembrada en el campo,
una linda amapolita
que has inspirado este canto."

Amapolita Morada

Lastly, the sixty to seventy miles of cruel desert north of Los Vidrios had to be crossed in order to reach Interstate 8, and many immigrants had perished or simply disappeared trying to make that extraordinary trek. Without being able to resupply with water en route, the way I knew I could on the longer Sonoyta-to-Gila Bend route, it would be nearly impossible to photograph the struggles of others. Most of my energies would be devoted to carrying the minimum six gallons of water it would take to survive such a dangerous journey.

That left me with the option of using either El Sahuaro or La Joyita, forty kilometers west of Los Vidrios, as possible rendezvous and departure points. I decided on El Sahuaro for several key reasons: It was reported to be the most popular departure point for crossing this remote desert. And depending on the group's angle of travel, it was no less than forty but not more than seventy miles to Interstate 8, and I knew the general locations of waterholes from which I could resupply, if I made the decision to use them. Finally, the proprietor of the restauraunt agreed to help me—once a book of my photographs convinced her I was not an American undercover agent.

Situated sixty miles east of San Luís Río Colorado and eighty miles

Starting line. Seen from the air, the remote outpost of El Sahuaro Café along Mexico's Highway 2; stretching east into the horizon across the frontier of Sonora, Highway 2 parallels the U.S./Mexico border and is the starting line for many illegal immigrants' race against death.

west of Sonoyta, in a merciless blast of desert between El Gran Desierto to the south and the Camino del Diablo to the north, El Sahuaro Café bore no resemblence to Tijuana as a border crossing staging area. Consequently, I was forced to hole up at the remote truck stop for two days and nights in the sweltering heat before I got my chance to cross America's killing ground with Mexican strangers.

The sun hung low in the sky, igniting the craggy southern flanks of the Tinajas Altas Mountains with golden fire, when an Estrella Blanca bus rumbled to a stop in front of the dusty outpost. Someone was getting off; I couldn't see clearly because the green and white bus blocked my view. But my heart raced the thirty seconds it took the bus to resume heading west toward San Luís Río Colorado, Mexicali, and Tijuana. When the heavy black plumes of diesel exhaust finally cleared, I saw four men heading north into the desert. There was no signpost, no trail, no welcoming committee promising forty acres and a mule if they survived, nothing but a narrow arroyo which served as a gateway to their dreams or their deaths. They were all carrying telltale one-gallon plastic water jugs. So I ran across the highway through the desert after them. What a strange sight that must have been: being chased by a lone *Americano* while they were still in Mexico. They were startled. So I quickly pulled a 35mm transparency out of my pocket. It was as small as a postage stamp, but they could clearly see the sun-bleached skull as I held the tiny white picture frame up to the hot blue sky. I explained I was a photojournalist, and that I wanted to show Americans how dangerous their journey was. "*Por favor, permitanme acompañarlos*" (Please, let me go with you), I asked them. They looked me over, no doubt wondering if I had what it took to cross the desert; they spoke quietly amongst themselves for a few minutes, then agreed to let me join them.

"*¿Permitanme?*" (Permit me?), I asked them. "*Tres minutos*" (Three minutes), I said, holding up my fingers. They nodded, hid in the brush, and waited for me to return. I ran back across the empty highway, grabbed my camera bag and three of the four one-gallon water jugs I had waiting in the back room, and waved goodbye to Estela Cordoba, the brown-eyed proprietor.

"*Adíos.*"

"*Díos te bendiga*" (God bless you), she wished me, and went back to mopping the cement floor with pungent Pinesol.

I started out the back door, but the water was not enough to cross forty to seventy miles of Sonoran Desert in the summertime. So I stood in the back room chugging the contents of a fourth gallon of water, gagging and vomiting until I drained the plastic jug.

That's how our ordeal began, my stomach bloated with water as I ran back across the only highway that crossed the desolate frontier of Sonora. But that's not how our ordeal would end. Not for Guillermo— and not for the rest of us.

Out of water and far behind, Guillermo enters the killing ground alone.

"Ten to twelve miles from the second body, I encountered a
third body. This body was buried under rocks, and a crucifix,
but I could see the skeleton."

Carlos Cobarubia Mesa

It seemed apparent what was going to happen next. In the parlance of
Border Patrol trackers, Guillermo was about to "go down." And records
show when someone in a group does go down, the others will leave him
behind to try and get help. But in this 4,100-square mile Empty Quarter, there are few practical landmarks to key off of. To the untrained
eye, the region's distant sierras and intervening desert valleys all whirl
together in a bad dream of scalding rocks, ankle-burning sand, and
skin-ripping cactus and brush; for its victims, the will to live is tortured
into submission by scorching heat, blurred vision, and legs paralyzed
by dehydration and fatigue. So it often happens that the victim can't be
rescued on time—if he's found at all. It's now apparent Guillermo is not

The skeleton-littered wastes of America's killing ground. Photograph by
David Roberson, from the John Annerino collection.

going to make it without help. I aim the long black lens, burning my fingertips on the hot metal as I follow-focus his deadly dance: he is limp-
ing across this thankless desert in a pair of cheap, rubber shower sandals
because he is saving his good shoes, his old tennis shoes, in a bag for a
job interview at a melon farm; he is out of water and falling farther and
farther behind, lost in a mirage of desperate hope. The motor-drive
whirs; I must show the struggle, but I must also go back and help. Suddenly, the group stops. Fear for their friend masks their weary, sunburned faces. No one is going to let Guillermo dance to his death alone.
They wait. They ply him with water. And, if need be, they will carry him
out of this desert—or die trying.

Guillermo slowly recovers, and we continue trudging across the
burnt crust of this desert which now simmers between 140 and 160 degrees Fahrenheit. The heat radiates through the flimsy soles of our
shoes, but Rosario feels it the worst. He is wearing plastic-soled, metal-
cleated baseball shoes, and he hops from foot to foot like he's walking
on hot coals. Worse, we each start draining the last of our water in hopes
of extinguishing the fire underfoot. My plastic water jug is the next to

run dry after Guillermo's and, after my last hard swallow of hot putrid water, I too start falling behind. The only reason I know this is because the group is growing smaller and smaller in the distance, as the shimmering mirage slowly engulfs their four tiny figures. I have run ahead of them far too many times to photograph their struggle, and now I am spent, and I am alone.

If Rosario was the tireless point man, however, Armando was the eyes of the group. His gaze pivoted back and forth across this dreary desertscape of creosote brush, withered cactus, and glaring sand with the piercing vision of a raptor on an unending search for the telltale dust-devil that would warn him La Migra was about to swoop down on us. I see that again, in the distance. Through my lens, Armando senses, then sees, that I've fallen impossibly far behind. Everyone stops to wait. I struggle to reach them, standing in a phantom mirror of cool water, but my legs and feet now burn with each footstep . . . and, then, before I realize it, the precious communal jug of water is thrust in my face by the same Mexicans who, gringos had warned me, "will slit your throat for your water." I wave away the burlap-covered jug, telling them *"No necesito, compadres. Gracias."* I will not drink another man's water in a desert where life has often been measured in mouthfuls. But their camaraderie spurs me on. We are indeed a group. It is then I realize we are going to make it across this hell on earth together or go down trying.

But suddenly Armando stops dead in his tracks: *"La Migra,"* he whispers, pointing far to the west. A white single-engine Super Cub drones huge, lazy circles near the foot of the distant Baker Peaks, and abruptly Armando, Rosario, Guillermo, and Marcelino scatter to the four winds across a broiling expanse of the Mohawk Desert. I stand there for a moment, wondering who to follow. I start after Armando, then turn and chase Rosario a quarter-mile back through the white heat. We collapse under a creosote bush—hacking and coughing up dusty red sputum—and wait to see if La Migra is tracking us. No doubt Dave is flying today. Like Joe, he's a skilled and dedicated "manhunter," and I've grown to trust and like them both. But Dave and Joe obviously haven't cut our sign. They're too far west, undoubtedly "tracking up" another group of "wets," as they like to call the men I'm with. In the next moment, the small airplane turns west into the sun-bleached horizon. When it does, Rosario sighs with relief—La Migra is gone. But when I watch Dave fly away in his Super Cub, I realize I'm watching the last practical option for a rescue disappear. Rosario stands up and waits for Armando, Guillermo, and Marcelino to regroup with us. But we are not going to make it.

A hot wind licks at us, wicking away what little moisture remains in our heat-ravaged bodies, as we continue staggering across the heart of this killing ground. Visions of skulls and bones that I've photographed the weeks before now come back to haunt me. We are out of water, and our empty jugs dangle uselessly at our sides. It will only be minutes before the heat drags us down, each of us, one by one. We will then crawl, on our bloody hands and knees at first, then just slither jerkily along until the life slowly burns out of each of us, or we simply go mad. It's all there in the Yuma County Sheriff's Department Incident Reports, the historic journals, the eyewitness accounts, the grisly polaroids. One of us will have visions of water and die from choking on mouthfuls of hot sand rammed down his throat. Someone else will try to slit his own throat with the edge of his belt buckle. Someone else will strip and stare naked at the sun until it burns the eyes out of his head. And someone else will rip up the earth around him with the bloody claws of his fingers in a deranged search for water. The lucky one, though, if he doesn't strangle himself in a barbed wire fence, or hang himself from the thorny limbs of mesquite tree, will simply lie down beneath the harsh shade, make peace with Tata Dios or beg the Virgen de Guadalupe for forgiveness, and wait for his scorched, shriveled lungs to squeeze out his last foul breath. But the desert will claim each of us, I feel it coming now, far from our loved ones. Our stomachs will swell, then explode in the heat. The vultures will gorge themselves on our rank carrion. The coyotes will then tear the legs and heads off our sun-jerked bodies. Our white skulls will stare up from the floor of this great desert.

My head is spinning, my body convulses with chills and nausea, and the ground is heaving at me in dizzying waves of sand and rock, when Marcelino first sees Interstate 8: "*¡Mira! ¡La carretera!*" (Look! The highway!) The salty white rime of dry sweat burns my sand-whipped eyes, so I can only make out the illusion of what we all now hope will be the end. But I run forward, stumbling as I do, hoping to capture the last punishing footsteps of these brave men.

I lie down on my stomach and bring down the long lens as they struggle toward the Interstate. Dots whirl before my eyes, and the heat sucks the air out of my chest, but the motor-drive whirs as Rosario, Armando, Marcelino, and Guillermo finally escape the desert they cursed as El Sahuaro.

We have been the lucky ones, I know now, as I clench the hot steering wheel with both hands, my once lean legs now hideously swollen with edema, and my body so deprived of fluid I will not urinate for another two days. Because no matter how hard I drive, there is still no escaping this droning, deadly heat. At this very moment, men are still marching north; like me, four of them have quenched their thirst by drinking from a toxin-tainted irrigation pipe near Interstate 8 in hopes of reaching Aguila, another hundred miles distant. But south of this demarcation line, in the black hole of the desert night, men—perhaps even their women and children—are quaffing their own urine in a desperate attempt to find a better life. Or any life at all. Because there is still no escaping the molten heat, or the blast of furnace winds which roar through the open windows of my pickup as I drive faster and deeper into America's killing ground.

Stoop labor. Rosario picks weeds in a west Phoenix lettuce field.

† 4 †

EL DORADO

†

"How sad it is to see a man,
when he is absent,
when he is absent,
when he is very far
from his mother land.
Especially when he remembers
his parents and his home.
Oh, cruel destiny, I begin to weep."

Alejandro Fernández
Paso del Norte

I T WAS THE JOURNEY that would never end.
For me, it could not end—the haunting memories of bleached bones and bloated corpses, the smiling faces of hungry children and the baleful eyes of lonely wives could not be purged until this saga saw print.

For Rosario, Marcelino, Armando, and Guillermo, it would not end until they reached the new El Dorado. Or they died trying.

Two hours after we escaped with our lives from the burning sands of the Mohawk Desert, they invited me to walk north with them another hundred miles to Aguila. It would be easier, they told me; there were plenty of irrigation ditches to drink out of along the way. With cameras dangling off my neck and shoulders, however, I could no longer pass for the migrant worker I once had. Years ago, I had been caught in a Border Patrol roundup of illegal immigrants in a Yuma melon field with two high school friends. But that was another time. After witnessing what Rosario, Marcelino, Armando, and Guillermo had endured in hopes of feeding their families—walking fifty miles across the merciless Arizona

69

desert in 24 hours—I was reluctant to do anything that might jeapordize their chances of getting work—even if it meant sacrificing the opportunity to get another set of important pictures.

So once we slipped out of the desert, four of us rested in a jojoba bean field a mile south of Interstate 8 while Marcelino snuck up to an irrigation spigot and filled our jugs with water. When he finally returned, we lay there in the festering heat till nightfall, guzzling cool toxic water before we parted ways. They walked northwest torward the Interstate under a canopy of stars, and I walked northeast toward the rush of glaring headlights. I didn't have to wait more than five minutes before I caught a ride with two drunks.

"What the *hell* you doin' out in the middle of no-goddamn-where with all them damn cameras?" The driver yelled at me. "Counting bighorn sheep," I yelled back over the thunder and rattle of his rotten muffler, "for the Game and Fish."

"Get on in," he yelled, chugging a beer with one hand and fishing into the twelve-pack between him and his dozing buddy with the other.

I climbed into the back seat of the old Buick. It was a road whale and a beater. The back floor was littered with empty Old Milwaukee beer cans. A kewpie doll bounced up and down behind me. And the upholstery was rotting and vomiting brown foam from two decades of baking in the Arizona sun.

"Where'd you say you was headed?" The driver asked. In the harsh light of the overhead dome, I could see he had weary blue eyes, he was missing two front teeth, and his matted grey hair was covered with a sweat-stained ball cap that looked like it'd seen the inside of a dumpster. He wore four days of grey whiskers and a torn white t-shirt that reeked of sweat, old beer, and fastfood droppings that spilled down the front of it like pigeon shit.

"Gila Bend." I said. *"Home."*

"Countin' sheep with all them damn cameras. Ain't that a hoot. How many you'd see?"

"Lost count."

"My name's Willie," he said, offering a hand that felt like a Gila monster crawling out of a tinaja of spittle and warm beer. "This here's . . . Never mind. He's too goddamned drunk to remember his name. So why'n the hell should I remember it for him?"

Good thinking.

As headlights rocketed past us, Willie careened back onto Interstate 8, dragging a tailpipe along the hot pavement that showered our escape with a roostertail of white sparks. Apart from being smashed, Willie seemed harmless enough, but I kept my eye on the rearview mirror and my hand on the door handle—wondering what it'd be like to roll out of this sled at seventy miles an hour if things got nasty. At least he was headed to Gila Bend.

As the lights of Dateland, Aztec, and Sentinel floated past, and the blast of hot winds roared through the open windows, my thoughts drifted back to Joe McCraw. When I first asked Joe if there was any way to show how dangerous it was for illegal immigrants to cross this immense stretch of desert borderlands, other than by accompanying a group to document their journey, he said no. But he also looked me in the eye, and with that good ole boy smile of his, he told me he'd catch me if I tried. I had little doubt about that. That's why I parked my truck in Gila Bend. I knew if Joe cut my sign and discerned the difference between my footprints and those of my companions, the first place he'd probably look for me would be holed up in Tacna's Chaparral Motel ten miles west of where we first hit the Interstate. I'd spent enough time with Joe slowly cruising Border Patrol drag roads in a four-wheel drive Ford Bronco, and cutting sign across the desert on foot, to know what a savvy tracker he was. Besides, he'd already caught one photographer barely twenty miles north of the border trying to cross the Tacna corridor with Mexican nationals several years earlier, and I got the distinct impression he'd be delighted to score another notch in his leather gun belt for me as well. A hundred miles southeast of Tacna, the Tucson Sector of the U.S. Border Patrol had the head of Geraldo Rivera on its spear for trying to cross Organ Pipe Cactus National Monument with an ABC-TV crew and ten illegal immigrants. The fact that I slipped through the net probably had as much to do with Joe being off duty—I would learn later—as the speed with which we crossed the desert and the skill with which Rosario, Marcelino, and Armando brushed out our tracks.

Since it was Guillermo's first trip across the desert, he wasn't allowed to brush out for fear too heavy a hand with a creosote branch would be a dead giveaway to La Migra.

As spread thin as the handful of Tacna Border Patrol agents were for patrolling their sector of this 4,100 square-mile desert, agent Tom Mc-Call later told me he finally cut our sign south of the Interstate near the jojoba fields. Using a flashlight to read our footprints in the black sand, McCall worked the backtrack like a bloodhound until one set of footprints veered off from the other four. His best bet, he told me later, was to go after the group, then go back for the "solo walker."

It is 10:30 PM when Willie rolls to a stop in a storm of dust in downtown Gila Bend. "Sure ya' don't wan't a beer?" He says.

"Naw. Like to, but my wife'll just think I been whoring around in Mexico again. Thanks the same."

I fling my water jugs into a trashcan and hobble three blocks down the dark, narrow sidestreet to my pickup. Wondering if the heat has ruined my film, I slide my camera bag across the seat and turn the ignition. I breathe a sigh of relief when the motor starts on the first try. I head to the store. In this town, the grocery list is obvious: a bag of crushed ice, a six pack of beer, a six pack of root beer, a pound of corn chips, a can of hot sauce, and two plastic-wrapped death burritos.

I check into the nearest motel two blocks away. It's run by an East Indian who floats through the summer night like a moth. I ask him for a quiet room in the back. They're all quiet, he tells me. For good reason. Nobody stays in what's often ranked as the hottest spot in the nation during the summer by choice. Especially if the swamp cooler's not working. I've got the motel to myself.

I throw my bags on the bed, and amble into the shower. The cold water is hot, but at least it rinses away the sand, salt, and sweat which whirl down the drain like brown sludge.

I crack a beer and call my fiancée. "I'm out. I know, I love you, too. Don't worry. I'll call you when I get up . . . "

It's 1:30 AM; I'm wearing a wet towel around my waist, a wet towel around my chest, and a wet towel around my head, when I finally cave in to fatigue and pass out on the hot white sheets. Seventy-five miles west of me, Rosario, Armando, Marcelino, and Guillermo are lying in the hot sand under a mesquite tree when they're startled awake by a glaring beam of light; that's when Agent McCall arrests them ten miles north of Interstate 8. After crossing fifty miles of burning desert in a night and day, what normally takes other illegal immigrants who survive the journey two to two-and-a-half days to cross, they did not have the energy to keep marching thoughout the night, which probably would have put them beyond the long arm of La Migra. Later that same morning, they signed voluntary departure forms and were bused back to San Luís Río Colorado, Sonora, tired, hungry, and thirsty.

That afternoon, I finally crawl out of bed to chug the ice cold six-pack of root beer I'd been dreaming about throughout the long smoldering night. But it's sitting in a vat of hot water, dead cockroaches, and a lifeless plastic ice bag. I peer outside, but the white light blinds me, slicing through the dark room like lightening. I close the door, squint my eyes, and hobble to the shower. It's sundown when I finally escape from this historic Arizona resort town.

Two days later, I am on the candlelit patio of a posh, five star Scottsdale resort; a hot desert wind flutters through the towering palm tress, and a meteor shower rains white light across the dark pyramid of Camelback Mountain. I am slow dancing in the velvety arms of my fiancée, mesmerized by the hynotic sway of her hips, when I discover I'm unable to articulate an answer for the most oft-repeated question at the high school reunion: "So, what have you been up to lately?" Two hundred miles southwest of here, I would learn later, Rosario, Marcelino, Armando, and two other men they'd met from Las Gallinas dance in the sand around Border Patrol sensors while crossing the border again. This time, they run though the citrus orchards outside San Luís, Arizona, near Well #9. Guillermo stayed behind to recover from his first desert crossing. From Yuma, Rosario's crew hopped a Southern Pacific boxcar to the Mohawk Rest Area, a dozen miles east of where we'd first hit Interstate 8. Hidden from view, they walked the shallow railroad ditch across the sprawling desert of the San Cristóbal Valley ten miles east to Dateland. Once at Dateland, they turned north and hoofed it another ten miles to Red Mountain Ranch where they used a phone to call a friend; he drove them the rest of the way to Aguila.

A week after their tearful departure from Las Gallinas, Sinaloa, Rosario, Marcelino, and Armando finally reached America's modern goldfields. But nobody held a fiesta in their honor for surviving a journey that would have killed seasoned outdoorsmen, trained athletes, veteran backpackers, and long distance runners. They were not given new clothes, seed money, or a cushy job. Nor was it likely they'd strike the mother lode, as Don Francisco Salazar had during the 1850s California gold rush—not unless they became ruthless drug lords by murdering their way through the ranks of snitches, thieves, smugglers, assassins, and corrupt bankers, politicians, and police officials on the cash payroll of notorious border cartels.

With their endurance still waning after their grueling desert crossings, Rosario, Marcelino, and Armando wore the prints off their fingertips picking cantaloupes twelve hours a day, seven days a week, in the burning desert sun until the harvest was in. And as astonishing as it may seem to those who've never endured such rigorous work, there were no picket lines of angry gringo farm workers shouting them down for stealing their jobs.

It was another six months before I saw any of them again. The desert had finally cooled. And the death toll seemed to abate. But even with a map and an invitation, locating these border phantoms a second time around was no easier than the cat-and-mouse game I played at El Sahuaro the first time. When I finally received a letter from Rosario, he explained they'd been busted back to Mexico after the melon harvest and invited me to visit him there. But by the time I arrived in Las Gallinas, he and Marcelino had already headed north again. Several late night phone calls upon my return to Arizona led me to a migrant camp in Florence, and finally to another in west Phoenix.

The world Rosario and Marcelino had entered after repeated arrests and dangerous border crossings was as alien to them as immigrants first appeared to Ellis Island immigration officials when the term immigrants was first coined during the 1920s.

They had left a verdant river valley in Sinaloa for a desolate agricul-

Illegal immigrants
bathe in an insecticide-
ridden irrigation ditch
in the Harquahahla
Valley.

tural waystation in Arizona. Crops were watered by lifeless irrigation ditches, not by the lush Río Fuerte and seasonal rains called *las aguas* and *las equipatas* that spill down from the heights of the Sierra Madre. They had left poverty-stricken homes, filled with families, love, and tradition for poverty-stricken migrant camps filled with danger, uncertainty, and strangers from their own country. They had left a culture that paid respect to departed souls in *El Día de los Muertos* (The Day of the Dead), one that revered the miraculous appearance of the Virgin before Mazhua Indian Juan Diego in 1531 during *El Día de la Virgen de Guadalupe* (The Day of the Virgin of Guadalupe), and one that also revered—among many other saints' days—the resurrection of Jesus Cristo during *Semana Santa* (Easter Week). They had left behind ancient religious traditions for a modern society that worshipped the images of Hollywood, the

José Hernández.

NFL, NBA, and PGA. They no longer bought fresh fruit, vegetables, and meat at the *mercado* in the church plaza. They bought canned beans, shrink-wrapped hamburger, and processed food at the strip mall. They no longer ate hot tortillas made by their wives each morning at first light; they ate deep-fried chips from a plastic bag they bought from a stranger who spoke a language they barely understood.

They left behind the respect of a community that knew them as honest men who braved the American desert to feed their families for the scorn of a country that depended on their back-breaking labor but refused to see them.

They left it all behind because Mexico could not offer them, and 40 million others, the one thing they needed most to pull themselves up out of depths of poverty and despair: an honest job for an honest day's wages.

So did José Hernández. Born in Ciudad Chihuahua, Chihuahua in 1944, the tough campesino was one of the many strangers Rosario and Marcelino came to know in their dire search for the American dream. When I first met José, he was resting on a makeshift bed in Rosario's and Marcelino's ramshackle trailer. The bed was fashioned from a lice-infested mattress and a sheet of plywood supported by four empty barrels of insecticide. José lay there recovering from the eighty-five mile trek he'd just made from Agua Prieta, Sonora to Wilcox, Arizona. Over the course of two decades, José told me, he'd made the three-day trek across the Chihuahuan Desert to Wilcox fifteen different times. Once in Wilcox, he either hopped a freight to Tucson or rode a bus to Phoenix.

The lengths to which Mexican citizens have gone and the hardships they have endured to look for work in the United States are the stuff of Mexican legends and corridos; Luís and Julián's *El Desierto de Arizona* is only one. In part, it goes like this:

> "They left their land,
> a small town in Durango.
> They reached the border
> leaving everything behind.
> But what they were seeking
> was already close by . . .
> The sun begins to climb
> the heights of the sky.
> The vultures, cawing
> like creatures in heat,
> swoop to devour
> two men on the ground.
> The heat is infernal
> and a sad wail is heard
> 'We couldn't make it.'
> 'How I hurt my mother!'"

But no border crossings that I'd heard of were more extraordinary than those of José Hernández. His treks to Wilcox along the historic route of Geronimo and the Chiricahua Apache paled in comparison to the dangers and rigors he endured trekking one hundred twenty miles across the desert from Sonoyta, Sonora to the forlorn sweep of the Harquahala Valley. Over a four year period, José told me, he'd made the five-day trek four different times—each time during the blistering month of May when harvest work was most plentiful. It was during one such trek that José found that corpse hanging by a belt from a mesquite tree eight miles north of Ajo.

But nothing shook José more than losing a friend during an incredible three hundred fifty mile border journey across New Mexico several years earlier. José and two other men had crossed the border near Palomas, New Mexico and followed the infamous Chihuahuan Desert route long known as the *Jornada del Muerto* (Journey of the Deadman), into the high mountains of New Mexico. The Jornada del Muerto was pioneered by Spanish conquistador Juan de Oñate in 1598, and historians estimate 573 Spaniards and three hundred other travelers succumbed to thirst and the Mescalero Apaches while traveling the Jornada del Muerto.

The deadly desert jornada at their backs, José and his companions continued following the treacherous route to Santa Fé, confident they would find work making expensive adobe houses for wealthy gringos. It was somewhere in the high country, José told me, he wasn't sure where, they didn't even have a highway map, when they were attacked at night in their camp by a bear. If José's story was true, and he appeared to have little reason to lie to me, since I wasn't offering him anything more than a friendly ear, it was undoubtedly a black bear; the last grizzly bear killed in New Mexico was reportedly shot by Carl and Blue Rice in 1931. José and another companion ran through the dark woods, listening to the mournful wails of their *compañero* as the bear dragged him away screaming. José never saw or heard from him again.

As strange, tragic, and extraordinary a tale as it was, Rosario's and Marcelino's story was even stranger. As winter night rolled in over the black spine of the Sierra Estrella Mountains, red meat and green chilis simmered on the small stove, and *ranchero* played in the background, my companions delved deeper into their precious weekend cache of American *cerveza* and their memories of coming to America. I discovered

The Seasonal
Agricultural Work
cards of Rosario and
Marcelino.

Rosario and Marcelino hadn't needed to risk their lives to cross the American desert—at least not the last couple of times. They had enough documented work experience to qualify for SAW (Seasonal Agricultural Work) permits. But each time they were busted back to Mexico, immmigration officials failed to advise them of the fact.

What neither Rosario or Marcelino had until recently was the king's ransom needed to pay for their SAW cards. At the time, it cost $185 to register with the Immigration and Naturalization Service, $60 for a physical exam, $7 for photographs, $6 for fingerprints, and $100 to a notary who was in the business of gouging her own people. That $358 was the equivalent of six months' work in Las Gallinas, or a week of nonstop stoop labor during the summer melon harvest.

In the dead of winter, in the Valley of the Sun, migrant farm workers like Rosario and Marcelino were hardpressed to find enough work to live in lonely squalor seven hundred miles north of home. There was little money left over to send to their needy familes, and nothing left to pay for their SAW cards. Promises of near-indentured servitude had to be made so they could work legally in the United States. Yet Rosario and Marcelino did not ease their burden by collecting food stamps or welfare. They had walked across the killing desert to work, not to look for handouts. They were proud men, trapped in an alien nation's Catch 22: pony up, or get the hell out of Dodge. Meanwhile, their families stood the risk of disintegrating.

The plight of Rosario and Marcelino was not unique. What was unique was the test of will and stamina they endured to work in the United States, and the character they demonstrated once they arrived. Proponents of California's Proposition 187 insist illegal immigrants are an enormous burden to American taxpayers: you don't need to look far to see the rampant abuses of social welfare programs that fuel the anti-immigrant fervor that has swept eastward across the our nation from California to the halls of Congress. Opponents of Proposition 187, however, argue illegal immigrants contribute more in tax dollars than they take out. If they're anything like Rosario, Marcelino, Armando, Guillermo, and José, there's little doubt about that.

I'm not sure where Rosario and Marcelino are now. A late-night phone message passed on to me several years ago indicated Rosario had brought his family to the United States. Things were not going well. He was still suffering through the tasks Americans will no longer do. But it was still not enough to support a family, especially since they were all now living in the United States.

Hopefully, fortune has smiled on Marcelino. I don't know. He may finally be one of us, reunited with his family and enjoying the fruits of his labor and the rights and privileges of U.S. citizenship.

As for Armando and Guillermo, I hope fortune has smiled on them too, whether they're still in Mexico or here in the United States. But they could still be out there right now, struggling across America's killing ground. Or, God forbid, their bodies may have already been devoured by "vultures, cawing like creatures in heat."

Flying between saguaro cactus, Border patrol pilot Dave Roberson 'cuts sign' from the air.

† 5 †

MANHUNTERS

†

"I often wonder how in the world a guy can even think he can
come across that desert, walking thirty, forty, fifty miles . . .
but if that was the only way to feed my family, I'd sure be
trying to come up here."

Joe M. McCraw
retired manhunter
U.S Border Patrol

BLACK LENSES cover my bloodshot eyes. Tears roll down my
cheeks as I walk lockstep into the crowded church. There
are six of us, and we are carrying the charred remains of a mu-
tual friend.

"Im nomine Patris, et Filii, et Spiritus Sancti. Ahhh-men." The priest
begins his sermon, but the image of a burning man trying to escape a
fiery cockpit haunts each of us. I lose myself in thought: the stark
aluminum skeleton of a single-engine Christen A-1 Huskey is buried
nose-down in the sand four miles north of the U.S./Mexico border, and
the black corpse of a man smolders in the wreckage twenty minutes
from home.

Dave wasn't supposed to die, and I wasn't supposed to be a friend.
He was a veteran pilot with 9,000 hours of flight time, and I was a photojournalist struggling with the images of America's killing ground. He
was supposed to keep it in the air—floating over drifting sands, towering saguaro cactus and tiny footprints—and I was supposed to keep
my distance. But in pursuit of a story that drew little concern from di-
vided nations, I befriended heroic people on both sides of the border:

the men who risked it all in search of a better life, and the men who risked their lives trying to hold the line.

A lanky Texan with a Lone Star drawl, David F. Roberson was one of those quiet heroes. Even if I hadn't known him, you could see the lives he touched by the open weeping and muffled tears of family, friends, Border Patrol pilots and agents, INS officials, Marine personnel, and his Mexican wife. On this somber July morning a half hour west of where Dave, Maj. Bruce Lohman, and I once hoisted icy Mexican beers at the end of our trek across the Camino del Diablo, nearly five hundred people have gathered to pay their last respects to a man whose character they knew well. But we would do so kneeling and crying in front of a closed casket. Dave died doing what he loved, cutting sign from the air, but he took his last breath the way no one should: strapped into a burning plane and eating flames in a barren sweep of the Yuma sands.*

It wasn't the way a hero's life was supposed to end, and it wasn't the way the Border Patrol began. But this epic tragedy had its beginnings long, long ago . . .

The first immigrants to enter North America without papers were believed to be bison and mammoth hunters; these desperate refugees crossed the Siberian land bridge circa 11,400 B.C.E. (Before the Common Era) and adapted to a hostile land that stretched across two hemispheres. When Christopher Columbus "discovered" this New World in 1492, and Hernán Cortés landed in New Spain twenty-seven years later, an estimated six to sixty million native people were already living in what would become Canada, the United States, and Mexico. But Spanish, Italian, French, and English were not among the five hundred fifty languages the continent's first citizens spoke. They spoke what to foreign ears were strange-sounding, unintelligible dialects, among them Aztec, Maya, Apache, and Sioux. And as these indigenous nations tried to enforce their own immigration policies with sacred words of power, ritual ceremonies, feathered lances, bows and arrows, and finally Colt .45s

---

* One source recently reported Dave was decapitated by the impact and died instantly.

and Winchester carbines, they were overrun and slaughtered by European explorers, soldiers, missionaries, immigrants, and settlers. By 1910, the estimated five to ten million Native Americans once living in what had become the United States were "reduced," through brutal ethnic cleansing, to a population of 237,196. *Asshole WHITE Devils*

As early as March 3, 1875, however, the new Euro-Americans tried closing the door behind them. That's when Congress passed its first immigration law, which prohibited foreign convicts and prostitutes from entering the United States. Seven years later, a second immigration law was passed. Referred to in neo-colonial terms as the Chinese Exclusion Act, the law of May 6, 1882 prohibited the "yellow menace" from entering the United States. By 1891, the list of immigrants ineligible to enter this country included the neighbors at our doorstep. But many Mexicans living in the remote, sparsely populated frontier which stretched westward from the Gulf of Mexico to the Pacific Ocean saw no geographical or cultural distinction between the mountains and deserts that straddle the border. The oft-disputed, U.S./Mexico border was a political line, not a physical boundary, fought over and paid for with blood and gold. The 1847 American invasion of Mexico City, the 1848 Treaty of Guadalupe Hidalgo, and the 1854 Gadsden Purchase set the borders.

But by the turn of the century, many Mexicans still living south of the border began fleeing the hunger, chaos, revolution, and bloodshed of their country for the same new life European immigrants first believed was theirs for the taking in Native America's ancestral realm.

As early as 1904, the Commissioner-General of Immigration hired seventy-five men to patrol the United States 1,952-mile southern border with the Republic of Mexico. They were called Mounted Watchmen, and the qualifications were simple: each man had to own his own horse and have the *cojones* to stare down heavily-armed *Federales, Rurales,* renegades, bandits, and revolutionaries. In return, each Watchman was given $115 a month, a rifle, a pistol, and a badge, with standing orders to keep the Mexicans and Chinese the hell out: a nearly two thousand-mile-wide breach. One agent described his job as trying to patrol a circle of locked doors with no walls in between.

Many Mounted Watchmen were former Texas Rangers, and some

had their own way of doing things in a place as dangerous and unpredictable as the border. Few were thought to produce more remarkable results during the 1930s than an old Texas Ranger drafted out of retirement to stem the flow of illegal immigrants crossing the Río Grande from El Porvenir, Chihuahua to Ft. Hancock, Texas. Overrun with border bandits that still plague isolated hamlets and towns throughout America's borderlands, the white-haired Ranger disarmed and arrested over a dozen armed men one Sunday morning as they stumbled out of the Fort Hancock saloon, and he padlocked them by the neck to a logging chain. Author Mary Kidder Rak didn't say how many angry and frightened suspects and bandits were chained together with hangovers when she wrote *Border Patrol* in 1938, nor did she divulge the old Texas Ranger's name. But she did write that the Mexicans were held hostage for nearly twenty-four hours until poor villagers living south of the Río Grande returned the "horses, cows, plows, hens, tools, [and] wagons" their sons, brothers, and husbands were accused of stealing north of it.

Such methods of border justice were rarely questioned as long as they produced results.

With passage of the Volstead Act of 1919 and the Immigration Act of 1924, it soon became apparent that a posse of Mounted Watchmen could no longer hold the line against illegal immigrants, regardless of their means. Nor could they roundup all the thieves and murderers on the run from *Federales* and *Rurales*, as well as apprehend the burgeoning number of *contrabandistas* who smuggled everything from burro loads of candelilla wax, mescal and tequila, to wagonloads of Chinese immigrants. Funded by the Department of Labor Appropriation Act of May 28, 1924, $1 million was earmarked to establish the Border Patrol within the Bureau of Immigration.

Four hundred fifty men were hired to saddle up and patrol six thousand miles of remote border country that defined the northern and southern limits of the contiguous United States. Their impossible dual mission, which has not wavered to this day, was to uphold the immigration and anti-smuggling laws of the United States.

But smugglers have frequently out-gunned the Border Patrol, and illegal immigrants have nearly always out numbered them. In 1927, four

Border Inspectors discovered that fact while working a set of tracks one night in the brushy and rugged Atascosa Mountains of Arizona. On the run from Mexican soldiers, Yaqui warriors crossed the Arizona/Sonora border twenty-five miles west of Nogales, and carefully walked single-file in the same set of footprints, hoping to outfox Mexican troops. When agents finally came to the end of the two leather sandal tracks, they found an old Yaqui Indian hiding under a tree. A rifle cradled in his arms, and bandoliers crisscrossing his chest, silver-haired Domingo Lara stood up, whispered a few words, and the frightening shadows of forty-six other Yaquis, armed to the teeth, stood up and surrounded the stunned agents in the dark. Fortunately for the agents, they had the good sense to feed the legendary guerilla fighters. They'd been on the run from Mexican troops for three days without food. As a result, they were also offered political asylum.

While checking their ranks that same night, Inspector Kenneth Adams noticed a young boy polishing an ornate pistol.

"You have a beautiful gun," Adams remarked.

"*Si señor,*" the boy said. "I took it from a Mexican general."

"You are wearing a very fine hat," Adams said. "Did that belong to the general?"

"*Si señor,*" the boy said. "I took that from him also—after I cut off his head with my machete."

The stuff of border legend and folklore, such tales induced many young men to join a legion which still prowled the mythic West in search of dark-eyed, moustached *banditos*, and few were more feared or infamous than Chico Cano. During the 1920s, Chico Cano's gang terrorized Texas' Big Bend country with robbery and murder. They earned a reputation as "cutthroats" when Chico's most vicious henchman, Jesús Rentería, nicknamed *El Gancho* for the stainless steel hook he wore on one arm, held down postman Mickey Welch with two other bandits and slit his throat with a knife. That's when the Army Air Service and the 12th Aero Border Patrol entered the picture. Using Marlin and Lewis machine guns mounted on single-engine DeHavillands that pilots called "flaming coffins," they brought law and order to the Big Bend frontier after gunning down El Gancho as he shot it out with their planes from the back of his white horse.

In Santa Elena, Chihuahua, a young wagon driver pauses
in front of the adobe ruins of Pablo Acosta; born in this
frontier village on the banks of the Rio Grande/Río Bravo
del Norte, Acosta died on April 24, 1987 in a fiery
shootout with heavily armed Federal Judicial Police who,
after refueling their helicopters at the U.S. Border Patrol
airfield in Marfa, Texas, attacked the drug lord from
the American side of the river.

Dave Roberson was another Texan who had a hankering for the
border. He wasn't the first Border Patrol pilot, but he was one of the most
dedicated to saving Mexican lives.

Born in Comanche, Texas in 1941, Dave joined the Army right out

Border Patrol tracker
and manhunter Joe
McCraw.

of high school in hopes of seeing the world. While stationed in Korea, he became a military policeman and, upon his discharge, joined the Odessa, Texas, Police Department. Four years later, he was accepted into the U.S. Border Patrol and was assigned to West Texas' Marfa Sector. A notorious drug corridor between Ojinaga, Chihuahua and Ft. Stockton, Texas, once controlled by drug lord Pablo Acosta, Dave learned to cut sign on the elusive trail of black tar heroin, marijuana, cocaine, and illegal immigrants who moved through the tangle of narrow canyons and desert badlands that guarded the Río Grande's Big Bend.

But the soft-spoken tracker also had the wild blue yonder in his eyes, and after two years at Marfa, Dave rotated to Ft. Stockton where he began studying for his commercial pilot and instrument ratings. Flying on weekends, it took Dave fourteen years to rack up the 1,500 hours of flight time required to become a Border Patrol pilot. When he did, he was offered the Supervisory Pilot position in the 2,150-square mile Yuma Sector in Arizona.

That's when Dave's path finally crossed Joe McCraw's.

Once described as "leather faced" and "gravel voiced," you'd think Joe McCraw was a curled-up old cowboy boot turning to dust on the south forty. On the country, Joe's an easy-going man with a country boy smile. He prefers to slake his thirst with a metal thermos of black coffee and ease his hunger with crackers and canned beanies and weanies while cutting sign in the desert borderlands.

Born in Langley Field, Virginia in 1932, Joe lived in Wellton thirty miles east of Yuma. He was going to college parttime, and working two jobs to support his wife and four children, when he sat in on a Border Patrol recruitment lecture given by now-retired Yuma Sector Deputy Chief John Peccolo. "The more he talked about the Border Patrol," Joe told me, "the more I thought, 'Man, that sounds like my kind of job . . . It's all outdoors. You get paid for tracking people.'"

Joe applied for the Border Patrol, and after sixteen weeks at FLETC (Federal Law Enforcement Training Center), he began working out of California's Calexico Station, cutting sign on line watch and staring into the dark, creaky shadows of wooden boxcars on railroad check. Eight years later, he became First Line Supervisor at El Centro Sector headquarters, where he spent three years managing fourteen other agents before returning to the Tacna Station as Patrol Agent in Charge.

Tacna is onsidered a hardship post by most agents, who rotate out after a mandatory two years.* But it's where Dave Roberson, Joe McCraw, and a handful of other dedicated agents became law enforcement heroes. They weren't just "catchin' 'em and throwing 'em back." They were tracking down and saving illegal immigrants from the horrors of death by dehydration in a four thousand one hundred square mile area. Because nowhere else in the Border Patrol—or law enforcement in general—was the line between an arrest and a rescue so thin as it was in the Tacna corridor during the summer.

* Now located in nearby Wellton.

Border Patrol pilot David Roberson (left) and tracker Joe McCraw work a
trail together in the Tule Desert.

Today, the Border Patrol is comprised of nine thousand agents who
patrol eight thousand miles of land and sea borders in the United States
and Puerto Rico. For Chicano activists, Mexican citizens, and others dis-
mayed by the irony, Latino agents now comprise forty-one percent of the
Border Patrol's force which in 1996 was authorized by Congress to increase its ranks by hiring one thousand new agents a year through the year
2001. To the horror of its victims and human rights groups, however, the
Border Patrol is reported to have "one of the worst police abuse problems
in the country," a rogue agency, critics argue, that is accountable to no one,
not to impartial internal affairs reviews or public watch dog groups. In two
scathing reports, "Frontier Injustice" and "Crossing the Line," Human
Rights Watch has documented some of the terrible abuses by Border Patrol
agents of political refugees and illegal immigrants. The disturbing accounts
of murders, rapes, beatings, and intimidation, as well as the detention of
American citizens and harassment of American high school students, rival
the horror stories reported by Central American refugees in Tecun Uman,
Guatemala, who had the misfortune of being caught by ruthless Mexican
immigration officials patroling the Río Suchiate border between Chiapas
and Guatemala. But that is Mexico; this is the United States.

Foot print of an illegal immigrant.

In a democracy founded on the principals of liberty and justice for all, human rights abuses carried out against illegal immigrants by Border Patrol agents remains unsconscionable.

Since 1979, though, another Border Patrol record has been kept. It's not one you often hear about because there's no balancing the ledger of human rights abuses and bad press. But it does shed light on the good men and women who, every day, continue to face the impossible responsibility of trying to stop human waves of illegal immigrants who each year now number nearly 1.5 million people, as well as interdict the flood of cocaine, heroin, methamphetamines, and marijuana Americans demand and consume each year.* One tracking from the air, the other cutting sign on the ground, Roberson and McCraw—oftentimes working in tandem with other agents and pilots—used the ancient art of sign cutting, once used by Native Americans to track down game and Euro-Americans. As far as has been recorded, Border Patrol trackers have

---

*During the first eleven months of 1998, the U.S. Border Patrol reported apprehending 1,448,032 illegal entrants, a 2.5% increase from 1997.

Notched foot print of
Border Patrol tracker
Joe McCraw.

rescued 247 illegal immigrants from death by dehydration in Arizona during the 1980s alone.

Then, Dave and Joe always knew when they worked a trail together
during the killing season between April and October, there was a good
chance they'd save someone's life—if they could track them down fast
enough. One trail they worked together resulted in one of the largest
desert rescues in Border Patrol history.

On a blistering July morning in 1987, twenty-five illegal immigrants from
Culiacán, Sinaloa crossed the U.S./Mexico border at the remote truckstop
of Los Vidrios on Mexico's Highway 2. Translated to mean "the glassy area,"
Los Vidrios is a fitting description for the shimmering mirages burning
off the desolate, black scoria of the Pinacate Lava Flow that oozes north
from the border into the horizon. It was here that twenty-three men, led

Apprehension or rescue? Following a faint, elusive trail across fifty miles of desert, agents Joe McCraw and Tom McCall and pilot Dave Roberson, tracked down this trio and found them lying in the sparse shade of a palo verde tree; they were severely dehydrated and still clutching a half-filled jug of putrid urine they hoped would be enough drinking fluid to cover the last ten miles of burning sand in their desperate bid to reach Interstate 8.

by two coyotes, unwittingly entered the mercilesss *despoblado,* hopeful of finding good paying jobs in northern California's San Joaquín Valley that would enable them to pay the $400 due for the passage north.

But even before they headed across the lava, their journey had the makings of a desert tragedy. The two coyotes, working for a smuggling ring based out of San Luís Río Colorado, told the men Interstate 8 was a mere six hour walk north of the border. All they would need was a gallon of water each. After two days and nights of struggling through 114 degree temperatures, their water was gone. They were severely dehydrated, and they began to scatter wildly thirty miles north of Los Vidrios in an austere sweep of the bombing range cradled between the rugged flanks of the Mohawk Mountains and the distant volcanic upheaval of

Border Patrol pilot
and tracker Dave
Roberson.

the Aguila Mountains. Some of those who survived ate toothpaste, ripped apart fish-hook barrel cactus to suck on its acrid white pulp, or drank their own urine. One who did not survive slit his own throat and wrists in front of his *compañero* Martín Flores Rodríguez. Sixty-two-year-old Filemón García watched his own seventeen-year-old son die miserably before him, jerking and convulsing wretchedly in the hot sand.

Incredibly, two men managed to reach an old white school bus in the San Cristóbal Valley nearly fifty miles north of Los Vidrios. The bus was used by Marine pilots for bombing and strafing practice in the 2301 eastern half of the Barry M. Goldwater Range, south of Dateland. The men hunkered down in the scalding shade of the bullet-riddled bus and waited to die. Fortunately, Marine helicopter pilot Capt. James Silliman, co-pilot Capt. Bruce Barnes, and crewman Sgt. Frank White spotted the two men while on a training mission in the bombing range. They landed, administered first aid, and called in the dogs.

That's when Joe and Dave first picked up the cold, two-day old trail.

Strapped into his white Super Cub, Dave took off from the Yuma airfield and flew east into the burning white horizonline. Joe slid into his Ford Bronco and headed south from Tacna into the grim desert he had always loved. Supported by agents from Tacna, and additional agents and pilots from Yuma's 18-man DART, (Desert Area Rescue Team), the sweep of Border Patrol manhunters began working the backtrack south from the school bus, across the blistering San Cristóbal Valley, all the way to the border. Some of them raced the long odds of still finding anyone else alive by cutting sign on the Mohawk Drag, the Culver Canyon Drag, and the Vidrios Drag. And all of them combed the group's route between Los Vidrios and Aztec on Interstate 8 that at best estimates was seventy miles long and required a *minimum* of six gallons of water per person to survive.

The survivors must have felt they were witnessing a miracle when white wings spiraled down from the heavens as they lay gasping beneath the thin shade of creosote bushes. Then came the crunch of footsteps and the strange apparitions of men dressed in green floating toward them in the haze, wearing big sidearms and carrying jugs of sweet water that would wash away the bitter taste of cactus and urine.

Incredibly, the tiny figures of twenty-two men had been tracked down and rescued from a vast killing ground which ran to the horizon in every direction. Only three did not make it out alive. One died by his own hand in front of a friend; another died of thirst in front of his father; yet another died of complications in front of doctors.

It was not the last such rescue in America's borderlands, only the biggest. And if immigration laws do not change to accommodate America's dependency on migrant workers, it will hopefully not be the last rescue. In the jublilant aftermath of the official awards ceremony held in honor of thirty-two Border Patrol agents and three Marines who pulled off the stunning rescue, twenty-one Mexican men were bused back to Mexico and desperation, two coyotes were arrested and in-

Agent Tom McCall
cools down a young
tracker overcome by
the desert heat.

dicted, and two Border Patrol agents spoke quietly and proudly of the
real rewards of their work.

That's when I first entered America's killing ground. Sitting in the
cool pines of Prescott, Arizona, two hundred miles north of the border,
I marveled at the heroic Border Patrol rescue of twenty-three illegal
immigrants. Who were these man hunters, and how did they track
people down to save them in a desert all but their legion and their prey
had forgotten even existed? I had to find out.

From the Border Patrol horror stories I'd read and heard about, I ex-
pected the worst when I had my first face-to-face talk with agents Joe
M. McCraw and David F. Roberson over hot coffee in the Tacna cafe.

As their words and concerns for the plight of illegal immigrants trying to cross the Tacna corridor spilled out, I was drawn to their story, the killing ground, and those who crossed it. But as the ensuing week played out, so did the realization of the enormity of trying to photograph the epic story over such a short period of time.

I flew with Roberson fifty feet off the deck as he cut sign from the air. I stared into the white face of a sun-bleached skull two miles from a drink of water. I rode shotgun with Joe as he tracked the desert by four-wheel drive and then by foot. But nothing moved me more than the trio they tracked down ten miles south of Interstate 8, after following their faint, elusive trail for fifty miles across the burning sand. Lying in the grim shade of a paloverde tree, a man and two teenage boys huddled together in the sparse shade clutching a half-filled gallon jug of putrid urine between them. Was it an arrest or a rescue? I didn't know at the time. But as the trio climbed into the back of the green Ford Bronco, I stared south across the desert, into the impossible distance. I remembered a long-forgotten promise I'd made to myself one summer when I was a boy, and ran away from home. I was taken in and fed by illegal immigrants who hid behind dark bandanas that also protected their faces from the sun, and we picked cantaloupes side-by-side twelve to fourteen hours a day, seven days a week. Then and there, I promised myself I would tell the story of their struggle to reach America.

I didn't know it at the time, but as the desert blazed around us and we continued to sip our hot coffee in the Tacna cafe, I was making a personal commitment to follow this story for the next decade.

"It gives you a good feeling," Joe told me before his retirement in 1987, "to be able to find somebody down there who's really in trouble. Because you realize if you didn't track him up, he more than likely would have died in the desert."

Echoing Joe, Dave told me: "The greatest rewards of my work are the search and rescue efforts out there when we actually save people in the desert."

These were not the words of rogue cops who had crossed the line to mete out their own brand of frontier justice. They were the honest sentiments of dedicated manhunters who tracked people down through hell on earth, oftentimes from sunup to sunset, to make sure their footprints reached Interstate 8, and that they made it out of the desert alive—whether they arrested them or not. In one of our last conversations, Joe told me: "I have to admire somebody who will get out and walk thirty, forty, sixty miles just to get a job."

Sadly, Joe had to quit doing what he loved most when he faced the Border Patrol's mandatory retirement age of 55: "Just at the prime time," Joe said, "the officer could be doing the service a whole lot of good."

With the forced retirement of an old-line manhunter like Joe and the tragic death of another veteran pilot like Dave, I couldn't help but wonder as I drove home from the crowded funeral, back across the same burning desert I crossed on foot with brave men from both sides of the line, how many more lives will be lost without the safety net provided by veteran trackers like Joe and Dave.*

In the distance, a white single-engine plane slowly banks in the hot blue sky over the Camino del Diablo, as Jane Roberson scatters her husband's ashes and bones over the hardrock spine of the Tinajas Altas Mountains. The hot blast of the prop wash and desert wind whirls a gray plume of ashes and bones over the stony mountains.

---

* Two agents who spoke on the condition of anonymity took exception to the National Traffic Safety Board's conclusion of pilot error, and said Dave was flying such tight perfect cicles through the quiet air of the Yuma Desert while cutting sign that he flew back through his own prop wash, and when the plane flipped he was too low to pull out.

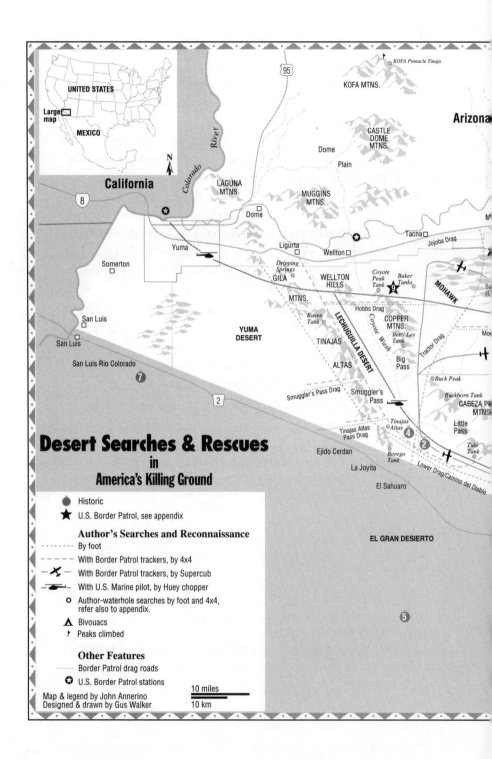

UNITED STATES

Large map

MEXICO

California

Arizona

KOFA Pinnacle Tinaja

KOFA MTNS.

CASTLE DOME MTNS.

Dome Plain

Plain

LAGUNA MTNS.

MUGGINS MTNS.

Dome

Tacna

Jojoba Drag

Yuma

Ligurta

Wellton

Somerton

Dripping Springs

GILA

WELLTON HILLS

Coyote Peak Tank

Baker Tanks

MTNS.

Hobbs Drag

Raven Tank

COPPER MTNS.

MOHAWK

San Luis

YUMA DESERT

Coyote Wash

Betty Lee Tank

Tractor Drag

San Luis

TINAJAS

ALTAS

Big Pass

San Luis Rio Colorado

Buck Peak

Smuggler's Pass Drag

Smuggler's Pass

Buckhorn Tank

CABEZA PR MTNS

Tinajas Altas

Little Pass

Tinajas Altas Pass Drag

Tule Tank

Desert Searches & Rescues

in

America's Killing Ground

Ejido Cerdan

Borego Tank

La Joyita

Lower Drag/Camino del Diablo

El Sahuaro

● Historic

★ U.S. Border Patrol, see appendix

Author's Searches and Reconnaissance

EL GRAN DESIERTO

- - - - - - - By foot

- - - - - With Border Patrol trackers, by 4x4

✈ With Border Patrol trackers, by Supercub

🚁 With U.S. Marine pilot, by Huey chopper

○ Author-waterhole searches by foot and 4x4, refer also to appendix.

▲ Bivouacs

⌐ Peaks climbed

Other Features

...... Border Patrol drag roads

✪ U.S. Border Patrol stations

Map & legend by John Annerino
Designed & drawn by Gus Walker

10 miles

10 km

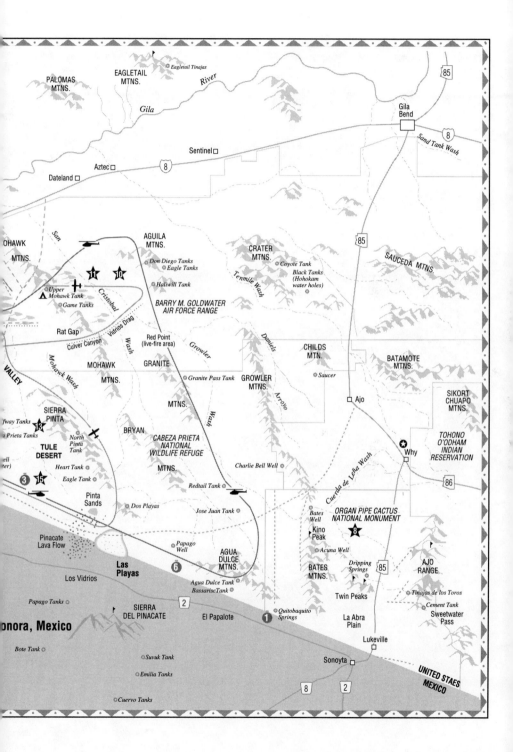

PALOMAS MTNS.

EAGLETAIL MTNS.

○ *Eagletail Tinajas*

River

85

Gila

Gila Bend

8

Sand Tank Wash

Sentinel □

Aztec □

8

Dateland □

OHAWK MTNS.

San

AGUILA MTNS.

CRATER MTNS.

○ Coyote Tank

SAUCEDA MTNS.

○ *Don Diego Tanks*
○ *Eagle Tanks*

Black Tanks
(Hohokam
water holes)

Tenmile Wash

85

△ Upper
Mohawk Tank

○ *Haliwill Tank*

Cristobal

BARRY M. GOLDWATER
AIR FORCE RANGE

○ *Game Tanks*

Vidrios Drag

Daniels

CHILDS
MTN.

BATAMOTE
MTNS.

Rat Gap

Culver Canyon

Wash

Red Point
(live-fire area)

Growler

SIKORT
CHUAPO
MTNS.

VALLEY

Mohawk Wash

MOHAWK

MTNS.

GRANITE

MTNS.

○ *Granite Pass Tank*

GROWLER
MTNS.

Arroyo

○ *Saucer*

□ Ajo

TOHONO
O'ODHAM
INDIAN
RESERVATION

SIERRA
PINTA

fway Tanks

a Prieta Tanks

North
Pinta
Tank

BRYAN

CABEZA PRIETA
NATIONAL
WILDLIFE REFUGE

MTNS.

Charlie Bell Well ○

Cuerda de Leña Wash

✪ Why

86

TULE
DESERT

ell
er)

○ *Heart Tank*

③ ⑮

○ *Eagle Tank*

Redtail Tank ○

Pinta
Sands

○ *Dos Playas*

Jose Juan Tank

○ *Bates
Well*

ORGAN PIPE CACTUS
NATIONAL MONUMENT

⑧

AJO
RANGE

Pinacate
Lava Flow

**Las
Playas**

○ *Papago
Well*

Kino
Peak

○ *Acuna Well*

Dripping
Springs

85

○ *Tinajas de los Toros*

Los Vidrios

⑥

AGUA
DULCE
MTNS.

BATES
MTNS.

Cement Tank

Sweetwater
Pass

○ *Papago Tanks*

SIERRA
DEL PINACATE

Agua Dulce Tank

Bassarisc Tank ○

②

El Papalote

①

○ *Quitobaquito
Springs*

Twin Peaks

onora, Mexico

La Abra
Plain

○ *Bote Tank*

Lukeville

○ *Suvuk Tank*

Sonoyta □

**UNITED STAES
MEXICO**

○ *Emilia Tanks*

8

2

○ *Cuervo Tanks*

The Mohawk Sand Dunes.

6

SEEING GHOSTS

†

"As the sun rose he sought the shade of a shrub
and there knelt in the final prayer for the dying;
then he laid himself down with feet and face
to the eastward, made the sign of the cross . . .
and composed himself for the end.
There . . . with the rising sun he died,
and his body lay lifeless under the burning rays."

W. J. McGee, 1906
on Pablo Valencia

THE HOT SAND scalds my ankles, the warm blood runs from my nose, and the haunting silence envelops me. The desert shimmers with mirages, as I lunge through the fiery heat of the great white dunes gulping in the hot air. I am running through a no-man's land, a bleak American wasteland forgotten by God and man, and I am looking, hunting, searching for any trace of evidence that will tell me somebody is out here right now—struggling toward a waterhole that glimmers in their thirst-ravaged dementia like a diamond in the sand.

Why am I out here, I wonder, wiping blood from the heat-seared membranes of my nose, the stinging sweat from my bleary eyes, the salt from my sun-cracked lips—running toward nowhere?

I am looking for the brave men who have marched north out of Mexico in search of the American dream, and I'm hoping to save just one of them. There is no explaining it to anyone else; I've had little success at that. I've simply been drawn here, to run across a smothering sweep of the Mohawk Sand Dunes in the remote chance I may find someone alive, someone who's had the extraordinary will and incredible stamina to keep struggling along a corridor of death that funnels survivors through a rocky breach in the Mohawk Mountains. But being drawn here is not reason enough to the handful of people who've listened to me, including my fiancée. So I tried explaining further: "Because they're out there dying right now." And then I quietly left town, unsure if this lonely search would bring me any closer to understanding why no one else seemed to care.

The great dunes draw me deeper, the white heat burns down on me as silver tow darts slalom and glimmer in the shifting sand. Creosote bushes burn gold then gray in the rising sun; the spindly arms of ocotillo wave in the furnace wind. But I see no one. Hear no one. Smell no corpses rotting slowly in distance. Nor do I see the reptilian tracks of dying men dragging their heavy legs and weary feet through the hot deep sand. There are no plastic bags blown up against creosote bushes, evidence that will point me to the suffering and the dying if I can follow the back track far enough—and still make it back to water alive myself.

There is nothing but silence and a luminescent white light that enshrouds a vast desert which patiently waits to swallow me alive if I stray beyond the point of no return.

I feel the hot wind burning the molting skin off my arms, and I decide to follow the trail of wind-blown sand; so I leave the faint two-wheel track I've been running on, and head southwest through the heart of the dunes. The heat-scorched membranes in my nose slowly cake with dry blood as I continue to suck hot air through my cracked lips. I pull coagulated strings of blood from my moustache and snort bullets of blood from my nose. I can breath freely again, but the heat continues to scorch my tender membranes as I spit red sputum out the side of my mouth.

In the distance, I see a *remolino* (whirlwind), hurling plumes of sand over the white granite teeth of the 2,950-foot Sierra Pinta. And with it I see, as I wipe the burning sweat from my eyes, the Lady in Blue. Her image still floats through the desert borderlands, leaving trails of blue flowers wherever she touches down. That's what the indigenous people of the Southwest believed, what they told the Spaniards who came through here later that a holy woman ministered to them and brought them the word of God in the playground of the devil. Padre Kino's escort Capt. Juan Mateo Manje wrote of her miraculous apparition after the now-extinct Halchedoma Indians told them that "a beautiful white woman dressed in white, gray, and blue, covered with a veil from head to foot, had come to these lands. She spoke to them and shouted and chided them in an unknown language. She carried a cross. They said the [Indian] nations of the Colorado River had shot her twice, leaving her for dead, and that returning to life she would fly away without their knowing where her home was. After a few days she would return . . . "

The indigenous people of New Mexico also spoke of the mythical Lady in Blue who saved one messenger from death on the Jornada del Muerto.

"He journeyed by north star, but the night became clouded and he lost his way, for he followed no trail, and he wandered about that night and far into the next night seeking water.

"By this time he was exceedingly tired and sore of foot, and was in such state that he was prepared to die. Then he saw before him the Blue Lady, beckoning him on. He stumbled along after her, and after awhile she stopped. When he came up he saw, beside her, a spring of fresh water, and he fell on his breast and drank his fill . . . And the spring is there today, Señor; the only water to drink that is to be found in the whole country of *la jornada del muerte* [sic]."

The Lady in Blue was later identified as Mother María de Jesús de Agreda, and when the renowned mystic was interviewed in Spain in 1631 by Fray Alonso de Benavides about her travels through the deserts of New Spain, the venerable nun said yes, she had ministered to the Indians of the Southwest. She had received a calling, and she traveled on the winds of God, the *remolinos* which whirl around me now like small tornadoes in a Kansas corn field.

My tongue grows coarse and sticky with saliva. My thighs burn from running in the blistering sand. My ears ring with silence. Only the *woosh-woosh* of my footsteps, the *hih-huh* of my breathing keep me companion in this living mirage. I turn, and head back toward the distant range which shields my lonely bivouac cave overlooking the only dependable waterhole for hundreds of miles around. I have crossed this desert with Mexican immigrants and know the suffering they have endured. I have struggled with companions in the footsteps of the forty-niners and glimpsed the suffering Sonoran goldseekers once endured. I have dogged Border Patrol trackers and witnessed the suffering they endured as they worked a set of elusive footprints in the noonday sun hoping to find their quarry before they died. I have trained for such long distance desert travel, running by the heat of day seventy miles a week, week in and week out, and still the distances seem impossible to me: forty, sixty, a hundred miles or more they must trek across the deadliest desert in North America. And still they come. Walking into the vast emptiness. Dreaming the golden dream.

And still they disappear.

The yellow sun burns flickering prisms of gold light over the horn of dark rock which marks the pass through the Mohawk Mountains. I run faster toward this ancient landmark, fearing I will be caught too far out in the killing ground without enough moisture or the benevolence of a miraculous apparition to return. In the specter of the incandescent yellow light, I see the dark silhouette of a deer hunter marching through the sand, and he is carrying the skull of John Doe Mexican to a highway patrolman's house. Coming from another direction, two Marines fall down in the sand near the corpse of John Doe Mexican; his feet and head are bound by black nylon cord. A California motorist stops on Interstate 8, and he sees the fully clothed skeleton of John Doe Mexican sitting upright under a mesquite tree; his "body lay lifeless under the burning rays." A Border Patrol tracker finds a pair of John Doe Mexicans, two of five young men who perished a half-mile from a drink of water, and his stomach turns when he sees "flies laid eggs in their eyes and mouths." Another photographs the mummified corpse of John Doe Mexican clutching the barbed wire fence bordering Interstate 8; his mouth was still open from the horror, because no one heard him gasping or saw him dying at the finish line to America's killing ground. Spin around in any direction, and there is no end to the terrible images of John Doe Mexican dying in the sand.

I run harder, trying to distance myself from the spirits. But what haunts me most is the image of eight Guatemalans disappearing. When their companions last saw them, they were foaming at the mouth, but trackers were forced to give up their search after monsoon rains erased all signs of their passing. Their ghost trail is followed a year later by the death march of eighteen other Guatemalans, including men, women, and children, who also vanished. Yet, there is no word in the national press of the disappearance of eight people, or even eighteen.

It is early morning when I reach the shade and safety of my cave in a dark cavity of the 2,775-foot Mohawk Mountains.

I'm hot, thirsty, and grateful I did not walk here originally, or run through the blistering heat and impossible distances to reach the 2,500 gallon water tank that feeds the desert bighorn sheep guzzler a hundred yards below. I was flown here in an olive-drab Marine helicopter three days and three nights ago, by someone who cared enough to listen. And as added security, Maj. Lohman dropped me off with ten gallons of fresh water for what I imagined would be a death watch and he knew would be a lonely bivouac.

My official reason for sitting in a cave in the buffer zone between the 2301 west half and the 2301 east half of the Barry M. Goldwater Range was that I would wait for desert bighorn sheep to come in, stressed from the June heat, and drink from the bee-infested sheep guzzler. That's what more than a dozen other people scattered throughout the neighboring Cabeza Prieta National Wildlife Refuge were doing right now. They were sitting next to shimmering pools of deep water waiting for the magnificent horned monarch to come staggering in to take a long hard drink. Then the sheep would be counted by all manner of these city dwellers, including naturalists, scientists, writers, and others who had money and time enough to do nothing but wait and watch. Long ago, the Sand Pápago, ancient nomads who once hunted the desert bighorn, revered its spirit by burning its bones in fiery cremation piles for blessing them with full stomachs in a land where lizards, mesquite beans, saguaro fruit, and *hía tatk* (sand roots) kept their gaunt stomachs from pinching their vertebrae.

I sit back on the hard black rock in the luminous heat.

The temperature will not abate until late September, when who knew how many more would die here, miles from home, a plastic jug of

Maj. Bruce Lohman,
helicopter pilot,
USMC.

water short of their dreams. My eyes droop closed with fatigue, and
even in the rocky shade I can feel the moisture fleeing my body: through
the breath I exhale, the skin caressed by the hot air, the bones scorched
by the black rock. I remember the first time I saw John Doe Mexican.
Dave dropped out of the sky and landed his white Supercub on a short
strip of glistening black malpaís to show me the bones: part of skull, a
jaw, a leg bone. But what struck me most was that the man died with a
quarter in his pocket and a flashlight in his hand a mere two miles west
of here and a life-saving drink of water. There was no identifcation, so
he was simply left where he fell in the Mohawk Sand Dunes.

I wept when I viewed his remains through the lens of my camera;
because his skull and bones weren't just a *calaca* (skeleton), that would
dance out the macabre and comical visions of millions of *Mexicanos*

who, each November, celebrate the Day of the Dead and sing songs like "Puño de Tierra":

> "The day when I die,
> I can't take anything with me
> But a fistful of dirt.
> Whatever happens in this world,
> Only the memories remain.
> Give happiness to happiness,
> Life is so quick to end."

I never discovered his real name. Nobody knows how many come in here. Nobody knows how many remain. And nobody knows how many escape.

The next time I saw John Doe Mexican, his skull was no more than a mile away from the previous one; he stared up from the black malpaís— his empty sockets fixed on his destination of Game Tanks not more than a mile away. I never discovered who he was either, where he came from, or whom he left behind. Nor did I discover the identity of John Doe Mexican who died a mile east of here; he was so delirious and exhausted from crossing the cruel desert from El Sahuaro to reach Game Tanks that he staggered right by two thousand five hundred gallons of water and died and withered on the black malpaís. The empty cans of *Jumex Papaya Nectar, La Costeña Jalepeños, Calmex Sardinas en Salsa de Tomate,* lime rinds, cracked plastic jugs of *Agua Purificada,* and other discarded remains like the red-checkered towel that once held a bundle of homemade corn tortillas, the ball cap stenciled with "Loreto Floats in the Sea," torn shirts, wing tips, and curled up tennis shoes are evidence that the phantoms of John Doe Mexican still come through here. I saw that yesterday afternoon, when I walked around the waterhole searching for clues to the identity of John Doe Mexican.

The last time I saw John Doe Mexican, I also wept. He was a bloated black corpse laying in the grim shade of a paloverde tree; his eyes were still wide open, staring at the sun that brought him down eight miles from a drink of water and five feet from a Border Patrol drag road. His stomach looked like it was going to explode; his flesh was rotting off his

face; and his black, sun-jerked hand was still reaching for his small transistor radio. I don't know what song he was listening to, but I hope it was a lively *cúmbia* that blessed him with a few pleasant memories before he died. But it could have been a sad corrido or ranchero song like "*Casas de Cartón*" by Marco Antonio Solis:

> "How sad it is to hear it rain
> on the cardboard roofs.
> How sad it is for my people
> to live in houses of cardboard.
> Children the color of my land,
> with the same scars from
> millions of stomach worms.
> And for that

The wave of a fatherless girl in Colonia Lazaro Cardenas, México.

> how sad it is for the children
> to live in houses of cardboard."

It is night. It is too hot to eat. So I scan the stations on my small radio, and listen to music from Juárez, Chihuahua to Tijuana, Baja California Norte, wondering who is spending a last night alive in a cantina, drinking and dancing with women they don't know before boarding a second class bus to cross the desert in the morning. How many of them have any idea what awaits them beyond the windowpane as the dark desert screams by? How many stand the remotest chance of crossing the gringos' strange killing ground? How many are sure candidates for the name John Doe Mexican, no matter how hard they pray in silence to Tata

Dios and the Virgen de Guadalupe? How many have no other choice but to flee their poverty-racked *colonias, casas de cartón,* and a beloved country gutted by corrupt politicians? With Mexico's unrelenting economic crisis, how many will come from the cloud forests of Pueblo and Michoacán, the jungles of Chiapas and Guatemala, the burgeoning colonias of Mexico City, Guadalajara, and Monterrey and don't even stand a remote chance of crossing a merciless *despoblado* that still kills tough campesinos from Sonora and Sinaloa who are accustomed to punishing physical work in a harsh desert climate? I drift off, then awaken when I hear coyotes howling in the distance and the footsteps of javelina crunching toward Game Tanks. Stars fade from brilliant white in the black heavens until they are consumed by the pink light of a dawn sky. I fire up my small gas stove, put a large metal cup on the blue flames, and dump a handful of coffee grounds into the tepid water. I lie back down on the hard black rock and wait for the coffee to brew. In a few hours, I will hear the whup-whup-whup of a UH-1N Huey echoing through the dry stony canyons of the Mohawk Mountains to whisk me away from this self-imposed vigil. There will be cold beer, homemade Sonoran-style Mexican food and cool white sheets to lie on with my fiancée. So I must leave this cave and have one last look for the doomed and the damned who continue to perish within sight of Game Tanks. Like Bruce, Dave would have understood.

Before his death, Dave Roberson expressed his deep concern for illegal immigrants who continue to die in the American desert. He suspected the actual number of bodies recovered might only be an indicator of a much larger death toll; and because of his concern, Dave took it upon himself to fly me throughout the Tacna Corridor to photograph skeletal remains of John Doe Mexican that had not been, or could not be, recovered without a helicopter. When it was possible to land his Supercub, Dave brought me face to face with the enormity of a tragedy that would have remained hidden and forgotten without his help. He was a dedicated manhunter, a Border Patrol tracker and pilot with human feelings. And contrary to the public perception of the Border Patrol, and my own jaundiced view of agents who cross the line or abuse their power, Dave was one of the good guys. Like Joe McCraw, and others

The discarded bra of a Guadalajara, Jalisco woman who was rescued by pilots and Border Patrol trackers on August 28, 1998; heat stroke victims often disrobe before death in a desperate attempt to cool off.

who work quietly behind the lines, they brought life to Mexican immigrants who would have perished in the American desert.

Even when circling fifty feet off the deck, however, a lifesize skull in the sand looks like a golf ball in a sand trap, and Dave died before he could show me them all. But in one of our last conversations before he crashed and burned, he started to sketch out a verbal map of where the others could be located so they could also be recorded. If they didn't have a name, or a pauper's burial, they could at least be photographed so people knew.

Without the eyes and wings of Dave, though, locating the missing remains was nearly impossible. Still, I went searching, and oftentimes I did not know why. There would be chopper flights with Maj. Lohman, an eight-day four-wheel drive waterhole reconn with Bill Broyles, and many searches on foot, alone. That's why I was out here now. Yet, each of these forays did not always produce the desired results; when they did, the remains always proved disturbing to me, as did the interviews, historical accounts, incident reports, and grisly polaroids. And as the death toll mounted, one question repeatedly reared its head.

How many people actually died out here, crossing this 130-mile stretch of the nearly two-thousand-mile-long U.S./Mexico border?

W.J. McGee was the first to address the futility of trying to answer that question. At the turn of the century, he wrote: "The roll will never be written in full, since most of the unfortunates left no records, scores leaving no sign but bleaching bones." For the historic era of the Camino del Diablo until 1900, estimates range from four hundred to two thousand dead. The period from the turn of the century until the end of the Bracero Program in 1964 remains a mystery, as does the fifteen year period between 1964 and 1979, when the Yuma Sector of the U.S. Border Patrol started keeping a Desert Death file.

The death toll for this seventy-nine year period may be no less staggering than that of the Camino del Diablo, but it remains a blank page in this chapter of American history. Yuma Sector Border Patrol statistics for the 1980s list sixty dead, and thirty-five missing; their figures are based on remains recovered. Estimates by the Arizona Farm Workers, based on interviews with migrant workers, put the death toll at three hundred for the same decade. In a published interview, however, Pima County sheriff's deputy Sgt. Joe Jett of the homicide dvision said: "For every national that makes it, there are probably at least ten that don't." If Sgt. Jett's estimation is correct, that would put the modern death toll in the thousands for Arizona alone.

Certainly the remains of thousands of victims would seem to leave trails of bones no less eerie and easy to locate than those encountered by early travelers on the Camino del Diablo. In 1856, Lt. Nathaniel Michler wrote: "All traces of the road are sometimes erased by the high winds sweeping the unstable soil before them, but death has strewn a continuous line of bleached bones and withered carcases of horses and cattle, as monuments to mark the way." But gone is the lure of one prin-

Flying with Maj. Bruce
Lohman and Rescue-1,
a Marine Corps
helicopter crew on
a training evolution
above the Gila
Mountains; pictured,
Naval corpsman Noel
Ramirez rides a stokes
litter tethered below
UH-1N Huey.

cipal trail like the Camino del Diablo that funneled large groups of travelers to the life-saving waterholes of Tinajas Altas.

The modern Caminos del Diablo are numerous, and range from the faint trails that cross the south Texas brushlands north of Laredo to the stony paths that snake through southeastern California's Chocolate Mountain Aerial Gunnery Range. Consequently, trackers face long odds and many obstacles when trying to locate a missing person. Principal among them is the sheer scope of the killing ground that in southwestern Arizona comprises a four thousand one hundred square mile no-man's land, and to the east encompasses the daunting expanse of New Mexico's and Texas' Chihuahuan Desert, and to the west includes the grim reaches of California's Colorado and Mojave Deserts. Compound the vastness of the American desert borderlands, its austere rugged terrain, and its sparse population, with the fact that remains are often covered by sand, decompose rapidly after summer monsoons and winter rains, are torn apart by coyotes, eaten by buzzards, remain hidden from view in arroyos or beneath paloverde, mesquite, and ironwood trees, and, of late, stolen by ghoulish collectors, and you have the characteristics of an Empty Quarter that has the ability to consume thousands of people over time without leaving any trace of them.

Some say one death is too many. Others: "They're just Mexican." What is the value of life in America today? A million lives were lost under Pol Pot's murderous regime in Cambodia before the world took notice; eight climbers die in a savage storm trying to climb the highest mountain in the world and it's emblazoned on the covers of national magazines; a princess dies in a car wreck, and a world of onlookers mourn. If a Mexican dies trying to cross the deadliest desert in North America, or eighteen Guatemalans vanish, and no one sees them, did they ever really exist in our national conscience? Mexico's ruling elite may be willing to sacrifice a poverty-stricken populace they still rule with the coldblooded ruthlessness of *conquistadores*, but how many Mexican lives will it take for American policymakers to take notice that they're still dying to work for us—and that they're dying on American soil? Or will only celebrity murders, terrorist bombings, and airline disasters make the headlines and network news?

Carrying this story alone for the last decade has been burden enough. It has ravaged my meager resources, broken dear relationships, and repeatedly tested my spirit and physical stamina to continue. It is time to pass the torch to someone else who also believes a single Mexican life is more important than a celebrity's latest bout in rehab.

I finish my coffee, lace on my running shoes and head south along the rugged flanks of the Mohawk Mountains toward Rat Cap. The air is still cool in the crimson, predawn light, and I scan the horizon for any telltale sign of movement. I learned from both Dave and Joe that, when it came to sign cutting, you couldn't follow a set of footprints and look for movement on the horizon line simultaneously. So I continue running, searching the horizon for someone, everyone, anyone, hoping I can reach them before their toe tag reads "John Doe Mexican." Or their flesh falls prey to the beak of Queléle.

BELIA RIP, Belia Rest in Peace.

The bloated corpse of "John Doe Mexican."

The bombed-out school bus in the Barry M. Goldwater Range's San Cristóbal Valley where the discovery of two Mexican nationals near death by a Marine helicopter crew on July 13, 1987 led to the rescue of twenty-two people by the Marines and Border Patrol trackers and pilots.

The skull of a Mexican national who died one mile after staggering by Game Tanks, used by immigrants who trek forty miles across the desert to reach it.

The charred remains of an F-14 A fighter jet serves as a grim reminder of the delicate balance between life and death in the desert borderlands.

The lower jaw bone of an illegal immigrant who died west of Game Tanks, two miles from a drink of water.

The abandoned bicycle of an illegal immigrant who may, or may not, have reached the life-saving water of Game Tanks below the peak three miles distant.

The wrist bone of a woman found at the mouth of Borrego Canyon two miles south of the historic waterholes of Tinajas Altas.

A burned-out van torched by a ruthless Mexican coyote who abandoned sixteen people, including one pregnant woman and two other women. He left them to cross sixty to seventy miles without water, experience, or knowledge of where they had to go; the group was spotted staggering across the desert by a wildlife specialist flying the no-man's-land on the edge of the Border Patrol's regular flight paths. The sixteen Mexican nationals from Guadalajara were saved on August 28, 1998.

The skull of yet another victim who died several miles west of Game Tanks.

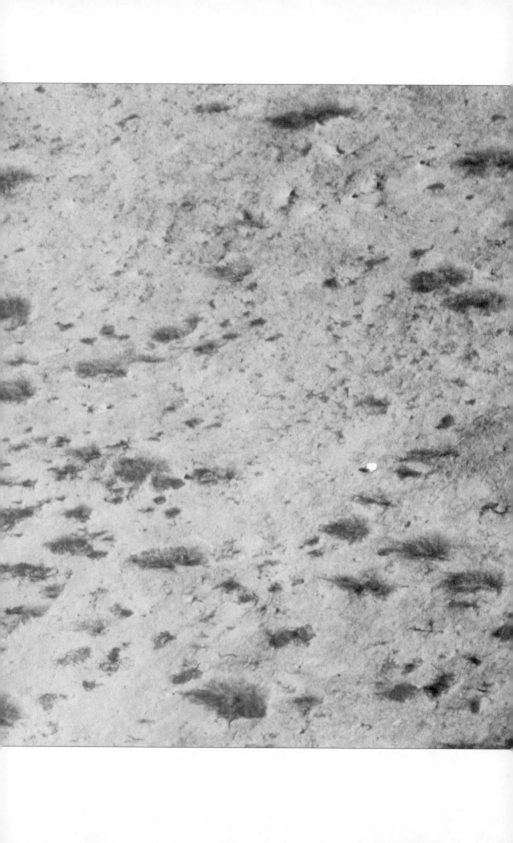

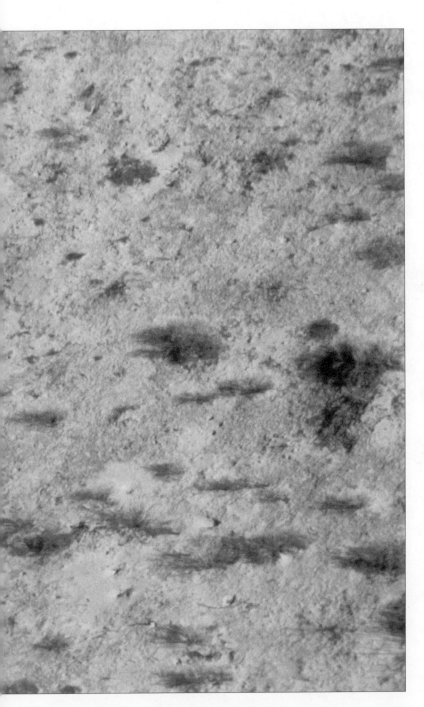

An aerial view of a skull in the Mohawk Sand Dunes is mute testimony of the difficulty of locating many who have perished trying to cross America's desert borderlands.

Mummy with a half-gallon jug of urine found in Dripping Springs Canyon, Gila Moutains. Photograph by David Roberson, collection of the author.

Illegal immigrant found dead near the Pápago Wells Road. Photograph by David Roberson, collection of the author.

The mummified body of John Doe Mexican ripped apart by coyotes. Photograph by David Roberson, collection of the author.

Many women in Mexico, such as Guadalupe López-Ruíz, have little idea their brave husbands have frequently crossed—and perished in—America's desert borderlands in hopes of feeding their families.

7

IN MEMORIAM

†

"It's much easier to know where you were born, than to know where you will die."

A saying heard in Colonia Ché Guevara, Mexico

AFTER STRUGGLING several hundred miles in the footsteps of Mexican immigrants, I started wondering if the United States and Mexico shouldn't build two memorials before the "tortilla curtain" is turned into the Iron Curtain: One border monument would be constructed in Sonora across from El Sahuaro on Mexico's Highway 2, and it would serve as both a shrine for families of the missing and deceased and as a warning to all those who think about crossing the killing ground; the second memorial would be built in Arizona at the Mohawk Rest Area on U.S. Interstate 8, and it would also include the names and dates of those who perished. It would start like this:

IN MEMORIAM

EN MEMORIA

This memorial is dedicated to the brave men, women, and children who died in search of the American dream. To desperate political refugees who fled hunger and oppression. To the dedicated Border Patrol trackers and pilots who often saved them. And to many others we'll never know . . .

† †

THE HISTORIC DEATH TOLL
*(SEE MAP INSIDE FRONT AND BACK COVERS)

†

"This is a grim land, and death dogs the foosteps of those who cross it."　　　　　　　　　　　　　Kermit Roosevelt, 1911

A Spanish-style grave marks the passing of an unknown victim in the Camino del Diablo region.

1. 1541, January 18: Spaniard Melchior Díaz dies near Sonoyta, Sonora. Twenty days earlier, Díaz had thrown his lance at dog that was bothering some sheep; the lance stuck in the ground, and when Díaz went to retrieve it his horse ran over the lance which pierced Díaz's abdomen. It is the first recorded death on the Camino del Diablo. IVES.

2. 1605, nsd: A mysterious and legendary woman known as both the Lady in Blue and the *predicadora*, "one who preaches," roamed the

desert borderlands preaching to indigenous peoples. Identified as Mother María de Jesús de Agreda, some historians believe she was murdered by Yuma Indians sometime after 1605. IVES

3. 1751, November 22: Jesuit missionary Enrique Ruhen is bludgeoned to death by Indians in Sonoyta during the Pima revolt. IVES

4. 1781, July 18: Padre Francisco Tomás Garcés is beaten to death by Indians during an uprising in Yuma; in December of that same year Lt. Col. Pedro Fages recovers the bodies of Garcés and Padre Barraneche, as well as the bones of Padres Joseph Moreno and Juan Díaz, who'd also been murdered by Yuma Indians. Fages transports the four bodies back across the Camino del Diablo for temporary burial in Tubutama, Sonora. IVES

5. 1800-pre?: Four Spanish-style graves mark the demise of an unknown party of desert travelers in the 1,838-foot Crater Range. RECONN

6. 1848-49, nsd: Between the fall of 1848 and the spring of 1849, an estimated 5,000 to 6,000 people left Hermosillo, Sonora for the California goldfields; many embarked upon the Camino del Diablo. It's not known how many thousands joined the exodus in the decade that followed, but by 1849 thirteen thousand of the estimated one hundred thousand non-Indians living in California were Mexican citizens. One can only speculate how many *Californios* died en route to California on the Camino del Diablo. VELA

7. 1850, spring nsd: Don Francisco Salazar is the first known traveler to describe the killing fields of the Camino del Diablo at Tinajas Altas: "The Tinajas was a vast graveyard of unknown dead . . . the scattered bones of human beings slowly turning to dust . . . the dead were left were they were to be sepulchered by the fearful sand storms that sweep at times over the desolate waste." BARN

8. 1850s, nsd: An estimated four-hundred people, many of them Mexican nationals, died of thirst on the Camino del Diablo during this decade; it's a record the International Boundary

Commission later wrote was "without parallel in North America." GAIL

9. 1855: The Camino del Diablo's death toll did not abate once California-bound immigrants reached Yuma Crossing. George Kippen encountered the bodies of many Mexicans between Ajo and the blistering sands of California's Colorado Desert west of Yuma. KIP

   July 9:

9-a. "Camped at 6 AM at Indian Wells. At sunrise passed the body of a Mexican a short distance from the wells who had died from thirst and exhaustion."

9-b. "At 5 PM . . . Passed 8 dead bodies on the road this day. Weather exceedingly hot, not able to travel in the day time."

   July 10:

9-c. "Camped at 1.30 AM. Left the Alamo wells at 5.15 PM for Cooks Wells. Passed the bodies of 1 Indian and 2 squaws."

   July 11:

9-d. "Camped at 2 PM. Left Cook Wells at 5.45 PM for Ft. Yuma. Passed the body of a Mexican who had been murdered.

   August 5:

9-e. "Arrived at the Playas at 9 AM Aug. 5. Passed the body of a Mexican who had died of thirst a short time previous."

10. 1857:

   January 14:

   "A Frenchman comes in a foot from the Tinajas Altas route to Sonora. Most horribly cut by 2 Mexicans who had murdered & robbed his 2 companions, but failed in killing him. He succeeded in saving his money, $800, but robbed his companions at 1,000 in gold coin."

   January 15:

10-a. "Yancy and myself went in pursuit of the 2 Mexicans who murdered the Frenchmen. Did not succeed in overtaking them, but found the bodies of the murdered men about 23 miles from Ft. Yuma. The most horribly cut men that I ever saw!! Burried them as well as circumstances would permit—and returned to Ft. Yuma."

March 22:

10-b. "Cario & Sacramento come from Sonoita. Dario reports the death of Marcelino by Apaches in the valley between the mines & Sonoita. Miscl: There has been all this month many Apaches in the valley & vicinity of the mines committing robberies & killing one of our peons."

11. 1857, April 18: S.N. Bunker and three other Americans were "shot like dogs" outside Dunbar's store by Mexican troops who crossed into the U.S. to seek retribution for Henry A. Crabb's expedition. Crabb's sixty-nine man contigent crossed the Camino del Diablo hoping to take Caborca, Sonora, but sixty-eight of Crabb's men were gunned down by locals in the dusty streets of Caborca. FORBE, GREEN and KIP

12. 1860's, nsd: A second goldrush during this decade claimed untold numbers of lives, but the exact death toll remains unknown.

13. 1861, July, nsd: A self-confessed murderer named Williams showed Raphael Pumpelly the grave of Charley Johnson on the Camino del Diablo; Williams told Pumpelly he murdered Johnson in a jealous feud over a Mexican woman and vowed he wouldn't rest till he "spit on his grave" a second time. PUMP

14. 1862, July 26: Union Army Sergeant George Hand described the resilient character of Sonorans who crossed the Yuma Desert: "On our arrival here [at Stanwix Station near Texas Hill] we found a Sonoran who had just returned from the Colorado [River] mines. Had been three days without water & 5 with out grub. He was nearly dead. He reported 14 more behind him and thought they were all dead. They, however, struck the river this morning. One drank so much water he died immediately. The others are here. We gave them some pinole. They looked very bad and were too weak to walk without help. It is an awful sight—makes one's blood chill to think of the hardship people are sometimes obliged to undergo." HAND

15. 1863, nsd: Sand Pápagos attacked three Mexican miners on the Camino del Diablo west of Sonoyta. One unidentified man was

murdered, but two others known as El Jabonero and Guastegui managed to escape. CEL and EZELL

16. 1864-1880s, nsd: The skeletons of eight people were discovered in California's Colorado Desert west of Yuma in April 1947 by surveyor Cleve H. Park; judging by the dates on the weapons found amongst the remains, Orion N. Zink concluded the victims were massacred in the Algodones Sand Dunes sometime between 1864 and 1880. ZINK

17. 1866 or 1884, nsd: Circle-of-8: Writing in 1896, Capt. David DuBose Gaillard described the tragedy of a family of eight Mexicans who died of thirst on the Camino del Diablo thirty years earlier. Gaillard wrote that their team of horses gave out and, while unloading their wagon, their glass water container broke—thus sealing the fate of the entire family. Thomas Childs however, later wrote that the family was murdered by the Sand Pápago in 1884. GAIL and CHILDS

18. 1871, nsd: The stone alignment NAMEER 1871 sits out in the middle of the Pinacate Lava Flow with three other stone alignments that might be graves: F, S, and E or BT. But the identity and fate of Nameer and the others remains unknown. TREK

19. 1871?: No less baffling is the name of Amalia S. Myers, etched into the black malpaís between the Mohawk Sand Dunes and the 2,775-foot Mohawk Mountains, discovered by Border Patrol pilot Dave Roberson; the identity and fate of Myers also remains unknown. AERIAL

20. 1872, nsd: John Killbright commited suicide when he took poison and jumped into the well at Mohawk Station. CRAMP

21. 1895, nsd: The remains of a sun-dried mummy were found in the desert near Gila Bend by two cowboys. The corpse was called "Sylvester" and displayed in a Seattle curio shop. AZHWY

22. 1896, nsd: Capt. David DuBose Gaillard of the International Boundary Commission was one of the first to estimate the number of people who died on the Camino del Diablo: "In all, four-hundred persons are said to have perished of thirst between Altar [Sonora] and Yuma in 8 years [during the 1850's],

and this scarcely seems an exaggeration, for the writer counted 65 graves in a single day's ride of a little over 30 miles." GAIL

23. 1890s, nsd: Sand Pápagos murdered two unidentified Mexicans at Quitobaquito Springs. CEL and HART

24. 1900, pre: James Kerrick and Lee Bentley, two bandits on the run from a Phoenix holdup, were killed by posse members at Sheep Tank in the 3,029-foot Growler Mountains. BROY

25. 1907, November 7: En route to the Sierra del Pinacate, the McDougal Expedition views the forlorn grave of a *cartero*, Mexican mailman, murdered by Indians, near the base of the 3,145-foot Puerto Blanco Mountains. HORN

26. 1907, November 10: McDougal Expediton member William T. Hornaday encounters two Japanese men who escaped with their lives from the Camino del Diablo west of Quitobaquito Springs; three other Japanese men from the ill-equipped party are believed to have perished in the Tule Desert. HORN

27. 1910, February, nsd: The body of an unidentified American was discovered at Las Playas by Sand Pápago Juan Caravales; coyotes had already mutilated the victim's body. LUM

28. 1911, August 11: Guided to Tinajas Altas by conservationist and bighorn sheep hunter Charles Sheldon, Kermit Roosevelt decribed the killing ground at Tinajas Altas: "A few hundred feet from the entrance [to Tinajas Altas], on the desert and scattered among the cactus, lie some 150 graves—the graves of men who have died of thirst; for this is a grim land, and death dogs the footsteps of those who cross it. Most of the dead men were Mexicans who had struggled across the deserts only to find the tanks dry . . . 46 unfortunates perished here at one time of thirst." ROOS

29. 1913, nsd: Deadman Gap. According to published accounts, an unidentified man died of thirst while trying to roundup his horses in the Crater Range; one anonymous source, however, reported the man was a Mexican bandit killed by an Ajo local in the name of frontier justice. BARNES

30. 1913, nsd: Dug sometime before the 1893 International Boundary Survey, Tule Well was the sight of at least two deaths. Two

men told Raphael Pumpelly they found and left an unidentified man in the well in 1913. On another occasion, an enterprising Mexican sold water at Tule Well until he was shot dead by a thirsty customer. PUMP

31. 1915, nsd: Harvard professor Raphael Pumpelly rode horseback across the Camino del Diablo in 1860 and, fifty-four years later, drove across it in a Model T Ford; the veteran Camino del Diablo traveler wrote: "It is a matter of history that more 2,000 persons have died of thirst and exhaustion on this part of the "Old Yuma Trail." PUMP

32. 1915, March, nsd: Two unidentified men died while trying to drive across Las Playas, and another man was rescued. PUMP

33. 1916, nsd: The body of prospector David O'Neill was found with his head in a mudhole. BRYAN

34. 1920, March nsd: The skeletal remains of a man and his burro were photographed in the Mojave Desert and given to Willard W. Erbeck, Sr.; the photograph and Erbeck's letter to the editor were published in *Desert Magazine* in December, 1964. ERB

35. 1927, June 23: Fugitive Wilbur Demming was killed in a shoot out with John Cameron and W.C. "Boots" Burnham at Bates Well. GREEN

36. 1928, nsd: Border Patrol agent Lon Parker was ambushed and murdered by Mexican fugitive Domitilio Ochoa in the 9,466-foot Huachuca Mountains; before dying, agent Parker managed to shoot and kill Ochoa's cousin, smuggler Narciso Ochoa, and his horse, (off map). RAK

37. 1930, September nsd: An unknown number of Mexican immigrants died of thirst on the Aberlardo Rodríguez Military Highway, (now known as Mexico Highway 2), which paralleled the Camino del Diablo south of the U.S./Mexico border. While patrolling the desolate, sandy track for the Immigration Service, Border agent and former Texas Ranger Jeff Milton and another agent named Nick Collaer got their car stuck in the sand and nearly died of thirst. En route to the Colorado River, Collaer said they saw "twenty-nine wrecked passenger-carrying au-

tomobiles . . . along the road . . . and the number of graves with articles of clothing and shoes of men, women, and children near." HALEY

38. 1937, July nsd: Civil engineers Jorge López Collada, Gustavo Sotelo, Jesús Sánchez Islas, and José Torres Burciaga died of thirst in El Gran Desierto when their truck got stuck in the sand while surveying a route for the Sonora to Baja railroad (Ferrocarril-Intercalifornia del Sur.) BROY and IVES

39. 1940, August nsd: Schoolteacher Gumersindo Esquer died of thirst near Sonoyta after a long desert journey on foot. Before Esquer died, he wrote his own epitaph on the rim of his hat: "I died of thirst through my own fault." HART

†   †

THE MODERN DEATH TOLL
*(SEE MAP INSIDE FRONT AND BACK COVERS)

†

"There's a hell of a lot of bodies out there we don't know about and probably never will."

Anonymous U.S. Border Patrol

40. 1941, August 6: Dateline Yuma. The *Arizona Republic* included the following story among page one headlines of World War II: "Seven Perish on Blistering Desert Road." "Yuma County Sheriff T.H. Newman said a Brawley, California family was returning from a visit to Santa Ana, Sonora when their truck got stranded in the sand 17 miles east of San Luís Río Colorado on the Aberlado Rodríguez Military Highway; that's where Francisco Arvallo discovered a grisly scene of suicide and death by dehydration four days after the family's ordeal began. Two members of the Cornejo family were rescued by Arvallo." AZREP

The deceased include:

1   Germán Cornejo, 52

2   Elías Cornejo, 25

3   Rafáel Cornejo, 17

4   Elisa Francisco, 4

5   Domingo Rocha, 26

6   Tomás Ponce of Santa Ana

7   Yocupicio of Santa Ana

41. 1960s, nsd: Authorities report California motorcyclists dig up historic graves and steal skulls for satanic cult rites. AZREP

42. 1962, nsd: In *The Thousand Mile Summer*, author Colin Fletcher described using what he called the "Wetback Trail" to cross the California's Colorado Desert northwest of Yuma; he also wrote: "I had heard of Wetback skeletons being found in remote canyons [of the Chocolate Mountains?] years after their owners had lost the way." FLETCH

43. 1964: Bracero Program ends; a file has not been uncovered which lists the death toll for the fifteen year period between the end of the Bracero Program and 1979, the year the Yuma Sector of the U.S. Border Patrol first started keeping a Desert Death file.

44. 1971, February 3: Carol Turner, 32, disappears while climbing the Sierra del Ajo in Organ Pipe Cactus National Monument; an extensive search by a 130-man team, including an Air Force helicopter, Pápago and Border Patrol trackers, and a psychic fails to locate her body. This search underscores the difficulty of locating a missing person in the desert borderlands. ABBEY.

45. 1973, October 4: Border Patrol pilot Freiderick "Fritz" Karl and Yuma Sector Supervisor John S. Blue both die when their single-engine Supercub hits a powerline near Tacna. USBP INTER

46. 1974, May 24: Five Mexican-Americans perish in the desert at Nine Mile Well south of Gila Bend when their employer, a "scrapper," abandons them while collecting brass shell casings in the Gila Bend Air Force Gunnery Range. AZREP and CAA

The deceased include:

1 Angel Contreras, 21
2 Frank Garza, 19
3 Robert Rodríquez, 20
4 Greg Avila
5 David Capistran, 19

47. 1978, August nsd: A 50 year old Sr. Flores of Col. Benito Juárez, Sinaloa dies while crossing El Sahuaro. RUÍZ INTER

48. 1978, August 15: An unnamed pilot died in the desert when his A-10 jet crashed in the Gila Bend Gunnery Range. CITI

49. 1978, December 13: An unnamed pilot died in the desert when his A-10 jet crashed in the Gila Bend Gunnery Range. CITI

50. 1979, August 29: An unnamed pilot died in the desert when his A-10 jet crashed in the Gila Bend Gunnery Range. CITI

51. 1980, May 20: The body of an unidentified Mexican man is found and left hanging by his belt from a tree eight miles north of Ajo; reported by José Hernández. HERNÁN INTER

52. 1980, July 5-6: Thirteen Salvadorans died in Organ Pipe Cactus National Monument, thirty miles north of the border and fourteen others were rescued by Border Patrol trackers and U.S. Customs agents. SFC AZREP, and CITI

The deceased include:

1 Sandra Huezo, 19
2 Rosa Huezo, 14
3 Claudia Huezo, 12
4 Carlos Rivera, one of the accused smugglers
5 *NI*   10 *NI*
6 *NI*   11 *NI*
7 *NI*   12 *NI*
8 *NI*   13 *NI*
9 *NI*

53. 1980, August nsd: 32 year old Gustavo López of Col. Benito Juárez, Sinaloa died while crossing El Sahuaro. RUÍZ INTER

54. 1981, Dec. 18: A deadman with a gold tooth is found near Dripping Springs in the Gila Mountains along the route from La

Joyita, Sonora to Wellton called *"El Cañon"*; there was a deep hole where the victim dug for water. RUÍZ INTER

55. 1981, July 9: The body of an unidentified 30 year old Mexican national was found under a tree in the desert east of Yuma thirty miles north of the border; twelve others were rescued by Border Patrol trackers. AZREP and STAR

56. 1981, July 11: The body of a second unidentified Mexican national was found under a tree in the same area earlier in the week by Border Patrol trackers. STAR and AP

57. 1982, spring nsd: A pilot and passenger were killed when their plane, believed to be carrying drugs, blew up over the Sierra del Pinacate, Sonora. HART

The deceased include:

1 NI

2 NI

58. 1982, July 11: The body of C. Juan Ceja Contreras was found by two Marines in the Yuma Desert. YCSD

59. 1982, August 2: A human skull with three teeth was found by a local man in the Yuma Desert. YCSD

60. 1982, August 30: The body of 33 year old Luís Guillen González was found by Border Patrol trackers fifteen miles south of Interstate 8 and three miles east of the Mohawk Mountains after he was reported missing by two companions on August 20. YCSD and STAR

61. 1982, September 3: The body of 25 year old José León Beltrán of Baja California was found by a Border Patrol tracker near Owl Station one mile south of Highway 80 at Milepost 52. YCSD

62. 1982, September 10: The body of 19 year old Tomás Torres of San Luís Río Colorado, Sonora was found fifteen miles south of Tacna after he was reported missing by his father. YCSD

63. 1982, September 17: *Excelsior*, a Mexico City newsaper, reported that eight people were believed missing in the American desert. U.S. Border Patrol Yuma field operations supervisor James Lockwood said: "We probably don't find most of those that die out there." STAR

The missing include:

1	*NI*	5	*NI*
2	*NI*	6	*NI*
3	*NI*	7	*NI*
4	*NI*	8	*NI*

64. 1982, September 18: The skeletal remains of a man believed to be an undocumented alien was found by Yuma County Sheriff deputies in the Mohawk Valley fifteen miles south of Interstate 8 on September 3. STAR

65. 1982, September 18: The body of "John Doe Mexican" was found beneath a mesquite tree by a California motorist 150 yards north of Interstate 8 at Milepost 52. YCSD

66. 1982, November 25: A human skull was found by a Yuma man fifteen miles south of Quartzite, 4½ miles east of Highway 95. YCSD

67. 1983, February 9: Human bones were found by a Wellton man between the Southern Pacific Railroad tracks and Texas Hill. YCSD

68. 1983, April 13: Human leg bones and a plastic water jug were found by a Wellton man in the Wellton Hills. YCSD

69. 1983, May 29: The bodies of two Mexican nationals were found by a Tacna man six miles south of January Farms. YCSD

    The deceased include:

    1 Bueno López Efraín, 26, of Los Angeles, Sinaloa.

    2 Madueño José Luís Navarro of Penjaro Nuevo, Sinaloa.

70. 1983, July 28: The body of 56 year old Rosendo Gómez Vásquez of San Blas, Nayarít, was found by a Border Patrol pilot nine miles south of Interstate 8 on Pápago Wells Road. YCSD

71. 1983, August 15: The body of an unidentified Mexican national was found by a Border Patrol tracker 1 mile south of Interstate 8 near Milepost 61. YCSD

72. 1983, August 22:

72-a. The Border Patrol recovered the skeletal remains of 12 people from an open grave in the Aguila Mountains. CITI

    The deceased include:

1	*NI*	7	*NI*
2	*NI*	8	*NI*
3	*NI*	9	*NI*
4	*NI*	10	*NI*
5	*NI*	11	*NI*
6	*NI*	12	*NI*

72-b. Twelve to thirteen other bodies reported south of Tacna had not been recovered. CITI

The missing include:

1	*NI*	8	*NI*
2	*NI*	9	*NI*
3	*NI*	10	*NI*
4	*NI*	11	*NI*
5	*NI*	12	*NI*
6	*NI*	13	*NI*
7	*NI*		

73. 1983, September 15: The body of Vicente Espinosa of Curevos, Mexico was found by a Border Patrol tracker 15 miles south of Dateland. YCSD

74. 1983, October 21: Human leg and arm bones were found by a Marine near Quarry Hill in the Yuma Proving grounds; one leg bone had a steel pin in it. YCSD

75. 1983, November 5: A human skull and bones were found by a snake hunter under a shade tree four miles northeast of Highway 95, near Milepost 33. YCSD

76. 1983, November 6: The body of unidentified 40 year old man, believed to be a Native American, or Mexican national, was found by a Tacna man at the Citrus City Water Tank 1½ miles south of Interstate 8. YCSD

77. 1983, November 9: The bodies of two Mexican nationals were found by a Border Patrol tracker 6 miles south of January Farms. YCSD

The deceased include:

1   Cornelio Alvárez Vela, 43, of Sinaloa
2   "John Doe" of Sinaloa.

78. 1984, June 3: The bodies of two Mexican nationals were found by a Border Patrol tracker 3 miles southeast of January Farms near Pápago Wells Road. Both victims had tried digging for water. YCSD

    The deceased include:

    1 "John Doe"
    2 Avila Joaquín Piñeda

79. 1984, June 25: The body of Francisco Avila-Herrera of San Luís Río Colorado, Sonora was found with a gourd water jug 11 miles south of Interstate 8 near the Game and Fish road. YCSD

80. 1984, September 7: A human skull was found by Marines in the Yuma Desert southeast of Marine Corp Air Station rifle/bombing range. YCSD

81. 1984, September 17: The body of an unidentified Mexican national was spotted by a Border Patrol pilot near Somerton. The victim crawled in circles before he died. YCSD

82. 1984, November 5: The body of an unidentified Mexican national was found with an empty plastic water jug by a Border Patrol tracker 4 miles southeast of Tacna. YCSD

83. 1984, November 9: The body of "John Doe" was found under a mesquite tree by a Border Patrol tracker 77 feet south of Interstate 8 at Milepost 40.6. YCSD

84. 1984, December 3: A human skull was found in a wash north of Hyder by an unidentified deer hunter and brought to a Department of Public Safety officer in Dateland.

85. 1985, nsd: A skeleton, with both feet missing, of an unidentified individual was photographed on the rocks west of Game Tanks by Border Patrol pilot David R. Roberson. ROBER

86. 1985, February 24: The skeletal remains of two people were found by ATC riders in the Yuma Desert; the remains of one victim were reported to be two months from the time of death, while the second victim was thought to have died a year earlier. YCSD

    The deceased include:

    1 *NI*
    2 *NI*

87. 1985, June 10: The body of "John Doe" was found by a Marine in the Yuma Desert at the Marine Corp Air Station; the victim's hands and neck were bound with black nylon cord and four plastic water jugs were found under a bush seventy yards away. YCSD

88. 1985, June nsd: A skull was seen 15 miles southeast of Tacna. RUÍZ, M. INTER

89. 1985, June 14: Lester L. Haynie, a 10 year Border Patrol veteran died when his single-engine Cessna hit a 500 KV power line in the California desert near Yuma. USBP INTER

90. 1985, June 16: The bodies of three Salvadorans were found by Border Patrol trackers 13 miles south of Interstate 8 near Pápago Wells Road; two others were reported missing. YCSD and GAZ
    The deceased include:
    1 Carlos Adalberto Martínez, 4
    2 Luís Edgardo Martínez, 5
    3 Rosario Soriano de Martínez, 21

91. 1985, June 21: The body of 30 year old Dora Alicia Meña of El Salvador was found by a Border Patrol tracker 4 miles south of Interstate 8; she was one of two victims reported missing from the June 16 group. Coyotes had already eaten her left leg, a grisly fact which underscores the difficulty in locating many victims. Meña's companion "Betti Jane Doe" was never found. YCSD

92. 1985, July nsd: The bloated corpse of an unidentified man was photographed under a mesquite tree west of Game Tanks by Border Patrol Pilot David R. Roberson. ROBER

93. 1985, July 8: The body of an unidentified 41 year old man was found in the Yuma Desert. FILE

94. 1985, July 18: The body of "John Doe Mexican" was found by U.S. Fish and Wildlife rangers near Christmas Pass in the Cabeza Prieta Mountains. The victim died with a plastic jug of urine and had set ten different fires in an attempt to signal for help or keep warm. YCSD

95. 1985, July 23: The body of 21 year old Arturo Castillo Ortega of Mexico was found by a Marine in the Yuma Desert. YCSD

96. 1985, July 30: The body of 58 year old Miguel Ruíz Juárez of San José Pama Huilitas, Mexico was spotted under an ironwood tree by a Border Patrol pilot 3 miles north of Rat Gap, 3 miles west of the Mohawk Mountains. YCSD

97. 1985, August 8: The body of 21 year old José Luís Casteñada-Mendoza of Col. Nazas, Durango, was found by Border Patrol trackers near the Mohawk Main Canal Levee. YCSD

98. 1985, August 29: The bodies of two Mexican nationals were found by Border Patrol trackers 3 miles north of Rat Gap. YCSD *The deceased include:*

    1 Rafáel Zamora, 26, of Salvatierra, Guanajuato

    2 "John Doe Mexican" of Salvatierra, Guanajuato

99. 1985, September 1: The body of a 35-40 year old "Unknown, Mexican Male" was found by a Border Patrol tracker 1½ miles south of Interstate 8 near Milepost 59. YCSD

100. 1985, September 8: A human skull was found in a wash beneath a tree by an ATC rider a half-mile south of Telegraph Pass in the Gila Mountains. YCSD

101. 1985, September 12: The body of 46 year old Ramón Flores López of El Tequezquite, Jalisco was found by a Dateland man 600-800 yards south of the Dateland school. YCSD

102. 1985, September 12: The body of 24 year old José Angel Sotelo-Muñoz of Ciudad Obregón, Sonora was found by a Border Patrol tracker in the San Cristóbal Valley 9 miles south of Dateland. YCSD

103. 1985, October 19: A human skull, tattered remains, and Mexican coins dating to 1979 were found by a Tucson man in the Pinacate Lava Flow. HART

104. 1985, October 20: A human skeleton was found resting in a sitting position, still dressed in a white shirt and long pants, by two hunters a half-mile north of Interstate 8 at Milepost 60. YCSD

105. 1985, December 4-10: 19 year old José Luís Rodríquez reported leaving three companions behind in the desert on August 28 after crossing the border at El Sahuaro. NEW

The missing include:

1   NI

2   NI

3   NI

106. 1985, December 9: A human jawbone was found by an Aztec man 1 mile south of the Red Mountain Farms office. YCSD

107. 1985, December 29: A human skull and bones were found by a Yuma man near the Fortuna Mine in the Gila Mountains. YCSD

108. 1986, nsd: Rosendo Vásquez died about 3:00 PM on the Pápago Wells Road south of Interstate 8. TIMES

109. 1986, February 21: U.S. Customs agent Glenn Miles is shot to death in the desert by Mexican drug smugglers when he "jumps a load" on the Pápago Reservation east of Ajo (off map). STAR

110. 1986, March 18: A human skull and bones were found in the desert 16 miles southeast of Tacna. CARR

111. 1986, April 21: During a 70 mile trek from El Sahuaro to Aztec, his 7th, Carlos Cobarubia Mesa of Sinaloa reported seeing three bodies; in a sworn statement made on May 1, he gave this report:

111-a. Body #1 was seen face down in the sand 17 miles north of the border.

111-b. Body #2 was found 12-13 miles from the first body and was wrapped in a white sheet.

111-c. Body #3, a skeleton, was found 10-12 miles from the second body and was buried under rocks. It's not known whether these bodies were ever recovered.

112. 1986, June 5: The body of "John Doe Mexican" was found under a mesquite tree by a Border Patrol tracker 15 miles southeast of Tacna near Big Pass. YCSD

113. 1986, June 9: The body of "John Doe Mexican" was found near a mine shaft by two campers on the north end of the Sierra Pinta mountains along Pápago Wells Road. YCSD

114. 1986, June 9: The body of "John Doe Mexican" was found under a mesquite tree by a Border Patrol tracker east of Mohawk Pass Rest Area, south of the Southern Pacific Railroad tracks. YCSD

115. 1986, June 24: A human jawbone and other remains were found by a Dateland man under a mesquite tree near Dateland. YCSD

116. 1986, June 25-26: Relatives reported that the body of 22 year old Roberto Miranda Ramírez was returned to Los Mochis, Sinaloa after he died in the desert several weeks earlier; Ramírez got lost and ran out of water while crossing El Sahuaro with two friends. FILE

117. 1986, July 25: The body of 41 year old Ramón Ramos García of Rancho Nuevo, Chihuahua was found by a Border Patrol pilot 12 miles south of Dateland. YCSD

118. 1986, July 29: The body of "Unknown/John Doe" was found by a Border Patrol tracker in the Yuma Desert 2 miles north of the border. YCSD

119. 1986, August nsd: The corpse of an unidentied man, viewed by an unidentified Border Patrol tracker, was photographed in the sand west of Vopoki Ridge by Border Patrol pilot David R. Roberson. ROBER

* 1987: Official reports requested for this year under the Freedom of Information Act were never received from the INS

120. 1987, or before: The remains of four Mexican nationals were photographed by U.S. Border Patrol pilot David Roberson and given to me in July.
    The deceased include:

120-a. *NI Mummy in sand* with right arm torn off and right leg eaten.

120-b. *NI Mummy on rocks* with half-gallon of urine in Dripping Springs Canyon, Gila Mountains.

120-c. *NI Man with eyes eaten out* under a mesquite tree.

120-d. *NI Man face down* next to survivor. Aerial.

121. 1987, July 19-25: An aerial survey of the Tacna corridor this week with Border Patrol pilot David Roberson produced photographs of the remains of five unidentified individuals believed to be Mexican nationals and one mysterious intaglio.

121-a. "Tacna skull" is photographed from the air approximately ten miles south of Interstate 8; unable to land due to sand.

121-b. A skull in the Mohawk Sand Dunes is photographed from the air approximately three miles west of Game Tanks; unable to land due to sand.

121-c. A second skull in the Mohawk Sand Dunes is photographed from the air near skull 121-b; unable to land due to sand.

121-d. Land and photograph a skull in the *malpaís* two miles west of Game Tanks.

121-e. Land and photograph the "Game Tanks Skull" on the *malpaís* one mile east of Game Tanks. The victim had apparently died after he reached the waterhole, but was so delirious and exhausted after struggling 40 miles to reach it he staggered right by it.

  * The intaglio *Amalia S. Myers* is photographed from the air on the *malpaís* between the Mohawk Sand Dunes and the Mohawk Mountains (see Entry 19); it's not known who Myers was or how she died.

122. 1987, June 20: The bodies of two Mexican nationals have been discovered in the desert near Ajo since April. STAR
The deceased include:
1   *NI*
2   *NI*

123. 1987, July 13: Two Mexican nationals died in the San Cristóbal Valley 15 miles south of Interstate 8, and a third victim died in a Yuma hospital; due to the heroic efforts of the Marines, Border Patrol trackers, and the Desert Area Rescue Team, 22 others were rescued from certain death. SUN
The deceased include:
1   Filimón García, Jr., 17, of Culiacán, Sinaloa
2   Ruebén Ruíz?
3   *NI*

124. 1987, July 18: The corpse of an unidentified man believed to an illegal immigrant was photographed under a mesquite tree by Border Patrol pilot David R. Roberson. ROBER

125. 1987, August 20: Border Crossing. I photographed a stone alignment on the trail from El Sahuaro at the U.S./Mexico border; it read BELIA RIP. While the identity of Belia is as baffling as that of Nameer 1871 and Amalia S. Myers, her fate was evident.

* 1988: Official reports requested for this year under the Freedom of Information Act were never received from the INS.

126. 1988, May 9: Two human skeletons are found west of Fortuna Mine, near Drippings Springs in the Gila Mountains. SUN and ROBER

    The deceased include:

    1 *NI*

    2 *NI*

127. 1988, June 27-30: Game Tanks Bivouac. Maj. Bruce Lohman flies me to Game Tanks in a Huey; a solo reconn of the area over the next 4 days produces no additional discoveries of human remains, though the "Game Tanks Skull" appears to be missing. When I mention this later to Border Patrol pilot Dave R. Roberson, he says he believes it was stolen by California RVers he'd spotted in the area the previous winter.

128. 1988, August 24: Camino del Diablo trek. I photograph five stone alignments believed to be graves:

    1 Stone Cross

    (see Entry 18, for 2 through 5 below)

    2 NAMEER 1871

    3 F

    4 S

    5 E or BT

129. 1988, August 25: Camino del Diablo trek. I photograph the Circle-of-8, a stone alignment of the family of eight who died of thirst, or were murdered by the Sand Pápago in 1884 (see Entry 17).

130. 1988, December 11-12: Mohawk Dune Traverse. Dave Roberson drops me off on the south end of the Mohawk Sand Dunes; a solo 16-mile long traverse of the dunes produces no additional discoveries of human remains; only discarded plastic water jugs are seen in the blowholes of this summer death trap.

* 1989: Official reports requested for this year under the Freedom of Information Act were never received from the INS.

131. 1989, April 1-2: Interviews conducted during the 50th anniversery celebration of the Cabeza Prieta National Wildlife

Refuge on the Camino del Diablo produced the following leads:

131-a. According to refuge manager, Dave Stanbrough, 12-16 skeletons were reported seen by a Mexican national under an ironwood tree between the Camino del Diablo and 2,217-Foot Sheep Peak on the southwest side of the Growler Mountains. *The missing include:*

1	*NI*	7	*NI*
2	*NI*	8	*NI*
3	*NI*	9	*NI*
4	*NI*	10	*NI*
5	*NI*	11	*NI*
6	*NI*	12	*NI*

131-b. Archaeologist Simon Bruder reported discovering remains, believed to be those of a mother and daughter, in Borrego Canyon 5 years earlier. MCAS recovered the remains at that time. During a visit to the site, I located and photographed what was identified as a wrist bone. *The deceased include:*

1 *NI*
2 *NI*

131-c. Bill Broyles reported U.S. Fish & Wildlife rangers found a body hanging on the Organ Pipe Cactus National Monument fence three years earlier.

131-d. Broyles also said the Cabeza Prieta NWR received a report from a Mexican national that another body was seen hanging in a tree near Palo Verde Camp in the northwestern corner of Organ Pipe Cactus National Monument.

132. 1989, July 14: David F. Roberson, a 23 year Border Patrol veteran died when his single-engine Christen A-1 Husky crashed in the Yuma Desert.

* 1990: Official reports requested for this year under the Freedom of Information Act were never received from the INS.

133. 1990, July 4: Waterhole Reconn. During an eight-day reconnaissance of waterholes in the Sierra del Pinacate, Cabeza Pri-

eta National Wildlife Refuge, and Barry M. Goldwater Range with Bill Broyles, I photograph a stone alignment spelling out "water" and four Spanish-style historic graves in the 1,838-foot Crater Range, (see Entry 5):

1 Circle Cross   3 Grave

2 Grave   4 Grave

134. 1990, July 5: During that same waterhole reconnaissance with Bill Broyles, I photographed the corpse of an unidentified Mexican national we discovered under a paloverde tree five feet east of the Copper Mountains' west side road, approximately eight miles south of the Mohawk Canal.

135. 1990, October 9: The body of 8 year old Jaime Ramírez was found by Cochise County Sheriff's deputies in the San Pedro River Valley 35 miles north of Benson after surviving alone for nearly a month, (off map). CITI

* 1991: Official reports requested for this year under the Freedom of Information Act were never received from the INS.

136. 1991, July 11: The body of 52 year old Francisco Hernández Morales of Tapachula, Chiapas was found in the desert 40 miles northwest of Tucson; survived by his 48 year Lacandón Indian wife Rosaura, the victim and his wife had walked 65 miles across the Baboquivari Valley when their *coyote* abandoned them (off map). STAR

137. 1991, August 15: The body of 20 year old Juan Carlos Martínez of Oaxaca was found by tourists on Puerto Blanco Road near Bonita Well in Organ Pipe Cactus N.M. 10 miles north of the border. CITI

* 1992: Official reports requested for this year under the Freedom of Information Act were never received from the INS.

138. 1992, June 2: Lt. Col. Edward E. Hackney, U.S. Air Force, died when his F-16 crashed 35 miles southwest of Gila Bend.

* 1993: Official reports requested for this year under the Freedom of Information Act were never received from the INS.

139. 1993, June 17: An unidentified 25 year old Mexican woman from Veracruz died in a Tucson hospital after being found by Border

Patrol trackers in the desert near Douglas 1 mile north of the border (off map). AZREP

140. 1993, July 6: The body of 20 year old Marco Antonio of Guatemala was found under a mesquite tree in the Aguirre Valley on the Tohono O'odham Reservation 50 miles north of the border; three men were rescued and told authorities eight men split off from their group and when last seen were frothing at the mouth (off map). AZREP and AP

141. 1993, July 10: Eight missing Guatemalans are feared dead in the Santa Rosa Valley, and an extensive search by Pápago and Border Patrol trackers, Pima County Sheriff's rescue team, and the Army National Guard is called off,(off map). AZREP and AP
     The missing include:

1	*NI*	5	*NI*
2	*NI*	6	*NI*
3	*NI*	7	*NI*
4	*NI*	8	*NI*

142. 1993, October 8: The bodies of two men authorities believe to be illegal immigrants were found in the desert west of Silverbell 60 miles north of the border (off map). CITI
     The deceased include:
     1-*NI*
     2-*NI*

143. 1993, December 2: The body of 21 year old Antonio Rodríquez Infante of El Ocuca, Sonora is found by his parents in the desert near Arivaca; the victim was walking back to Mexico with two companions when they reported him missing (off map). AZREP

  * 1994: Official reports requested for this year under the Freedom of Information Act were received incomplete from the INS.

144. 1994, June 24: 18 Guatemalans, including men, women, and children are reported missing in the desert 35 miles northeast of Sells; its not known if any survived, (off map). AZREP and AP
     The missing include:

1	*NI*	3	*NI*
2	*NI*	4	*NI*

5 *NI*	12 *NI*
6 *NI*	13 *NI*
7 *NI*	14 *NI*
8 *NI*	15 *NI*
9 *NI*	16 *NI*
10 *NI*	17 *NI*
11 *NI*	18 *NI*

145. 1994, December 1: The body of an unidentified individual was found in November by a motorist three miles north of Tule Well. INS MEMO

146. 1994, December 22: The body of an unidentified 64 year old man was found south of Wellton by Border Patrol trackers. INS MEMO

* 1995: Official reports requested for this year under the Freedom of Information Act were received incomplete from the INS.

147. 1995, September 28: Skeletal remains of an unidentified individual were discovered near the Baboquivari Mountains by a Border Patrol tracker (off map). INS MEMO

148. 1995, October 27: 73 year old Robert Harrison of Rye, Colorado died of thirst in the Sierra del Pinacate of Sonora thirty miles south of the Camino del Diablo; Harrison's brother-in-law, Donald Wages of Oklahoma City was near death when he was rescued after the five day ordeal. STAR

* 1996: Official reports requested for this year under the Freedom of Information Act were received incomplete from the INS.

149. 1996, May 15: The body of 30 year old Georgina Butriagos Antón of Lima, Peru was found in the desert 10 miles northwest of Douglas by Cochise County Sheriff's deputies (off map). USBP MEMO and STAR

150. 1996, June 14: The body of an unidentified Native American was discovered by Border Patrol trackers in the desert near Sells two miles north of the U.S./Mexico border. INS MEMO

151. 1996, June 15: The bodies of three Mexican nationals were discovered by Border Patrol trackers in a searing creosote flat a half-mile from a drink of water, seven miles south of Eloy; on

June 16, trackers found the bodies of two missing companions a half-mile away from the first three victims, and on June 21 they discovered the body of the sixth victim near Sil Nakya (off map). AZREP and USBP MEMO

The deceased include:

1   Gonzálo Olivas Cebreros, 34
2   Arcenio Olivas Cebreros, 29
3   Antonio Soto Muñoz, 21
4   *NI*
5   *NI*
6   *NI*

152. 1996, June 22:

152-a. The body of a Mexican national was found by Border Patrol trackers 8 miles south of Tacna. AZREP

152-b. A search was being conducted for the missing companion of victim 152-a. near the Tinajas Altas Mountains. AZREP

153. 1996, June 25: The body of an unidentified man was found in the desert near Arivaca by Pima County Sheriff's deputies, (off map). STAR

154. 1996, June 29: The skeletal remains of an unidentified man were found by Border Patrol trackers near Three Points, six miles south of Highway 86 (off map). USBP IR and STAR

155. 1996, July 1: The mummified body of an unidentified woman was found by a rancher near Douglas 1½ miles north of the U.S./Mexico border; it hasn't been confirmed whether or not the woman is María Florencia Fermiento-Bermao of Ecuador who was reported missing by her family and thought to have been the companion of Georgina Butriagos Antón who died in the desert nearby on May 12 (off map). USBP MEMO and STAR

156. 1996, July 3: The body of 19 year old Enrique Montera Torres of Querétaro, Mexico was found by Border Patrol trackers at Cameron's water tank near Ajo; Torres's two companion's told investigators they hid his body in the desert after he died from head injuries sustained during a car wreck after crossing into the U.S. illegally. INS MEMO

157. 1996, July 8: The body of an unidentified individual was found by Border Patrol trackers in the desert near Douglas after a woman filed a complaint with the Border Patrol. USBP COMPLAINT & MEMO

158. 1996, August nsd: Fourteen Mexican soldiers died of thirst in the desert near Laguna Salada, Baja California Norte (off map). IMPAR

* 1997: Official reports requested for this year under the Freedom of Information Act were received incomplete from the INS.

159. 1997, May 28: 29 year old Air Force Capt. Amy Lynn Svoboda died when her A-10 jet crashed in the Barry M. Goldwater Range southwest of Gila Bend. CITI

160. 1997, July 1: The body of 54 year old Roberto Urbano Torres of Vasco de Quiróga Ecueandero, Michoacán, Mexico was found in the desert near Why by Border Patrol trackers. STAR

161. 1997, July 1: The body of an unidentified individual was found by firefighters battling a brush fire on the U.S. side of the Colorado River. SUN

162. 1997, July 7: The body of a 25 to 35 year old woman investigators suspect was an illegal immigrant was found in the desert with empty water jugs one mile north of Douglas (off map). STAR

163. 1997, August 6: Eight Mexican nationals drowned in a savage flashflood while crossing the border between Agua Prieta, Sonora and Douglas, Arizona (off map). STAR

    The deceased include:

    1 Ivan Maldonado Vásquez, 16, of Santiago Teanguesoenco, México
    2 Juan Torres Morales, 21, of Santiago Teanguespenco, México
    3 Mario Bustos Romero, 21, of Tonatico, Guanajuato
    4 José Eloy Olmedo Solis, 18, of León, Guanajuato
    5 Rubén Gavia Ramírez, 23, of León, Guanajuato
    6 María Socorro Ramírez Pedroza, 34, of Mexico City, México
    7 Javier Castillo del Carmen, 28, of Temixco, Morelos
    8 Juan Manuel Ortíz Hernández, 19, of Michoacán.

164. 1997, August 6: 22 year old José Alfredo Chávez Godoy died of thirst while crossing the desert near Calexico, California (off map). STAR

165. 1997, January 1—September 6: Sixty-eight illegal immigrants died attempting to cross the Mexico/California border during this period; thirteen of the victims died while crossing the Mojave Desert. AZREP

The deceased include:

1	*NI*	8	*NI*
2	*NI*	9	*NI*
3	*NI*	10	*NI*
4	*NI*	11	*NI*
5	*NI*	12	*NI*
6	*NI*	13	*NI*
7	*NI*		

* 1998: January 1–December 31: More than 250 illegal immigrants died while crossing the U.S./Mexico border.

166. 1998, June 19: Ebelio López Laines of Veracruz, Mexico died in the desert north of Ajo. STAR

167. 1998, June 28: 22 year old Rosa Palomino Pérez de Cardeñas of Michoacán, Mexico died north of Nogales after being abandoned by her coyote (off map). STAR

168. 1998, July 13: The body of an unidentified man from Jalisco, Mexico was found in the desert north of Lukeville. STAR

169. 1998, July 25: 33 year old Raúl Mendoza of Colima, Mexico died in the Yuma Desert. STAR

170. 1998, July 25: 19 year old Sonia Soto Escalante of Guatemala died in the desert north of Lukeville. STAR

171. 1998, July 26: 16 year old Juan Ezequiel Gutiérrez Andrade of Michoacán, Mexico died in the desert near Palominas (off map). STAR

172. 1998, July 28: 20 year old Ana Claudia Villa Herrera of Veracruz, Mexico died in the desert east of Sells (off map). STAR

173. 1998, July 29: 23 year old Miguel Angel Vásquez Godinez died in the desert south of Arizona City (off map). STAR

174. 1998, August 20: 27 year old Elydia Martínez of Mexico City died in Tucson's St. Marys' Hospital from heat related causes after crossing the border near Nogales (off map). STAR

175. 1998, August 23: An unidentied 29 year old Mexican man died in the desert near Cowlic after crossing the border with his parents and three other companions (off map). STAR

176. 1998, September 1: Supervisory Border Patrol Agent Kenneth L. Smith reported finding the body of a Mexican national picked apart by buzzards in the Devil's Hills. No date was given. INTER

177. 1988, September 4: Supervisory Border Patrol pilot J. Howard Aitken found the body of a Mexican national in the Butler Mountains while cutting sign in the Yuma Desert. BROY

NE. 1999: An untold number of illegal immigrants will die in America's desert borderlands. They have yet to be identified. *The deceased and missing will include:*

1 *NI*	1 *NI*	1 *NI*
1 *NI*	1 *NI*	1 *NI*
1 *NI*	1 *NI*	1 *NI*
1 *NI*	1 *NI*	1 *NI*
1 *NI*	1 *NI*	1 *NI*
1 *NI*	1 *NI*	1 *NI*
1 *NI*	1 *NI*	1 *NI*
1 *NI*	1 *NI*	1 *NI*
1 *NI*	1 *NI*	1 *NI*
1 *NI*	1 *NI*	1 *NI*
1 *NI*	1 *NI*	1 *NI*
1 *NI*	1 *NI*	1 *NI*
1 *NI*	1 *NI*	1 *NI*
1 *NI*	1 *NI*	1 *NI*
1 *NI*	1 *NI*	1 *NI*
1 *NI*	1 *NI*	1 *NI*
1 *NI*	1 *NI*	1 *NI*
1 *NI*	1 *NI*	. . .

ABBREVIATIONS USED

Entries

NE New entry
NI Not identified
nsd No specific date

Historic Sources

AERIAL Aerial reconnaissance with Dave Roberson.
AZHWY *Arizona Highways*
BARN Barney, James M.
BARNES Barnes, William C.
BROY Broyles, Bill
BRYAN Bryan, Kirk
CEL Celaya, Alberto
CHILDS Childs, Thomas
CRAMP Crampton, John F.
ERB Erbeck, Willard W.
EZELL Ezell, Paul
FORBE Forbes, Robert H.
GAIL Gaillard, David DuBose
GREEN Greene, Jerome A.
HALEY Haley, J. Evetts
HAND Hand, George
HART Hartmann, William K.
HORN Hornaday, William T.
IVES Ives, Ronald L.
KIP Kippen, George
LUM Lumholtz, Carl S.
PUMP Pumpelly, Raphael
RAK Rak, Mary Kidder
RECONN Waterhole reconnaissance
ROOS Roosevelt, Kermit
TREK Camino del Diablo trek
VELA Velasco, José Francisco
ZINK Zink, Orion M.

Modern Sources

AP   Associated Press

ABBEY   Abbey, Edward

AZREP   *Arizona Republic*

CAA   Court of Appeals of Arizona

CARR   Carroll, Austin

CITI   *Tucson Citizen*

FILE   Desert Death File

FLETCH   Fletcher, Colin

GAZ   *Phoenix Gazette*

HART   Hartmann, William K.

HERNAN   Hernández, José

IMPAR   *El Imparcial*

INS   Immigration and Naturalization Service

INTER   Interview with author

IR   Incident Report

MCAS   Marine Corp Air Station, Yuma

MEMO   Memorandum

NEW   *New Times*

ROBER   Roberson, David

RUIZ   Ruíz, Rosario or Marcelino

SFC   *San Francisco Chronicle*

STAR   *Arizona Daily Star*

SUN   *Yuma Daily Sun*

TIMES   *Los Angeles Times*

USBP   U.S. Border Patrol

YCSD   Yuma County Sheriff's Department Incident Report

APPENDIX A

*Expeditions by Foot, Horseback, and Wagon
on the Camino del Diablo*

Arroyo del Muerto, Sierra del Pinacate, Sonora.

Before 1540: The *Hía Ced O'odham* (People of the Sand), band of Pápago first used the route to travel between nomadic camps and precious water holes known as *Tjunikáatk* (Where There Is Saguaro Fruit), Bates Well; *'A'alvaipa* (Little Running Water), Quitobaquito Springs; *Ótoxakam,* (Where There Is Bulrush) Tule Tank; *Tjukomókamtjúupo,* (Blackhead Pools) Cabeza Prieta Tanks; and *Óovak,* (Where the Arrows Were Shot) Tinajas Altas.

1540: Spanish commander Melchior Díaz is the first European to tra-

NOTE: (Refer to Map II on pages 4 and 5 to use with Appendix A).

165

verse the the Camino del Diablo and is also the first known person to die on it during a freak accident.

1699: Jesuit missionary and explorer padre Eusebio Francisco Kino and Lt. Juan Manje make the second traverse of the Camino del Diablo and provide one of the first eye-witness accounts of the Sand Pápago's desperate existence.

1771: Missionary Fray Francisco Tomás Garcés is the first European to traverse the Camino del Diablo mid-summer.

1774: Capt. Juan Bautista de Anza pioneers a new leg of the Camino del Diablo along the forbidding west side of the Gila Mountains.

1781: Ensign Santiago de Islas leads a small group of Spanish families across the Camino del Diablo to settle along the lower Colorado River.

1782: Lt. Col. Pedro Fages makes a return journey along the Camino del Diablo with the bodies of Padre Garcés and three other murdered missionaries.

1849-1900: Thousands of Mexican immigrants travel the Camino del Diablo to reach the California goldfields and settlements. During this time, when the Camino del Diablo earned its name, historians estimate between four hundred and two thousand people died traveling it, making it the deadliest immigrant trail in North America.

1854: Andrew B. Gray, Peter Brady, and a Texas Western Railroad survey crew travel the Camino del Diablo in June.

1855: Army Lt. Nanthaniel Michler and José Salazar survey the new international boundary for the 1854 Gadsden Purchase.

1857: Henry A. Crabb's ninety-three man fillibustering expedition follows the Camino del Diablo to Caborca, Sonora; all but one young man are massacred by irate locals who keep Crabb's head in a jar as a warning to other gringo fillibusterers.

1861: Harvard professor Raphael Pumpelly crosses the Camino del Diablo in July and escapes death when it rains at Las Playas.

1890: Godfrey Sykes and Charlie McClean are forced to trek from Punta San Fermín, Baja California Norte to Colonia Lerdo, Sonora after their small sailboat is destroyed by fire; Sykes later writes of this adventure in *A Westerly Trend.*

1891-1896: Capt. D.D. Gaillard and the International Boundary Commission surveys and marks the U.S.-Mexico border.

1905: Anthropologist William J. McGee camps at Tinajas Altas throughout the summer and later recounts the incredible ordeal of Pablo Valencia in his paper "Desert Thirst as Disease."

1907: William T. Hornaday, Daniel T. McDougal, Godfrey Sykes, Jeff Milton, and John M. Phillips explore Sonora's desolate Sierra del Pinacate region; Hornaday later writes of the expedition in *Camp-Fires on Desert and Lava.*

1910: Norwegian Carl S. Lumholtz explores the desert borderlands encompassing the Camino del Diablo and the Sierra del Pinacate region, produces one of the region's best maps, and later writes of his expedition in *New Trails in Mexico.*

1913: Hunter and naturalist Charles Sheldon climbs some of region's most rugged desert peaks and sierras; the diary of his travels is published posthumously in *The Wilderness of the Southwest.*

1917: Geologist Kirk Bryan explores much of the region in a vintage Ford touring car and produces a landmark U.S. Geological Survey paper, *Routes to Desert Watering Places in Pápago Country.*

1980: Sonoran desert historian and writer Bill Broyles retraces the route of Pablo Valencia during a solo mid-August trek, and later writes an account of his adventure in "The Ordeal of Pablo Valencia."

1983: Bill Broyles and Chuck Bowden retrace the route of the ancient Hohokam shell trail from Cholla Bay, Sonora to Ajo, Arizona.

1984: Bill Broyles retraces the 1907 route of the Hornaday/McDougal expedition west from Sonoyta, Sonora on a solo trek through the Sierra Pinacate to the Gulf of California and back.

1985: Bill Broyles and Chuck Bowden retrace Carl Lumholtz's 1910 route from Sonoyta, Sonora through the Sierra Pinacate to the Colorado River delta.

1987: Photojournalist Annerino crosses the Lechuguilla and Mohawk Deserts with four Mexican citizens on a mid-August border crossing.

1988: The Annerino-Lohman-Roberson party make an unsupported mid-August trek along the Camino del Diablo, linking the Yuma

Wagon Road, the ancient Camino del Diablo, and Juan Bautista de Anza's historic route.

1990: Enrique Salgado Bojórquez, José Manuel, and other Mexican *vaqueros* (cowboys) retrace the Camino del Diablo on horseback from Caborca, Sonora to Yuma, Arizona.

n.d.: Denver attorney Ron Hauver and two mules retrace the Camino del Diablo from Yuma to Organ Pipe Cactus National Monument during February.

APPENDIX B

Water Requirements for Crossing America's Killing Grounds

The cracked, empty water jugs of an illegal immigrant who may or may not have made it out of the desert alive.

Over the years, "experts" have erroneously reported that the fluid requirements for desert travel is a gallon of water per person per day. The grim realities, however, are quite different. Death by dehydration was the number one killer of immigrants and gold seekers struggling along the Camino del Diablo during the 1850s and 1860s and, to this day, it continues to be the principal cause of death for Mexican nationals trekking across America's desert borderlands.

The following chart, based on the author's 130-mile long mid-August trek across the Camino del Diablo, will hopefully shed some light on an individual's actual fluid requirements and why so many people continue to perish in America's desert borderlands.

DAY 1, 17 MILES, AJO TO BATES WELL, AUGUST 22.

Water carried: 3 gallons each.
Water consumed: 2½ gallons each.
Traveling time: 7 hours.
Hours traveled: 6:00 to 10:40 AM, and 12:30 to 2:40 PM.
Temperature maximum*: 106°F, with appalling humidity.
Permanent water: Bates Well.
Standing water: In washes between Highway 85 and Darby Wells, found
  but not used. (Numerous sand tanks, 2 to 5 gallons.)

DAY 2, 23 MILES, BATES WELL
TO PÁPAGO WELL, AUGUST 23.

Water carried: 4 gallons each.
Water consumed: 3 gallons each.
Traveling time: 9 hours.
Hours traveled: 6:00 to 11:30 AM, 2:15 to 3:30 PM, and 4:00 to 8:30 PM.
Temperature maximum: 106°F, with appalling humidity.
Permanent water: Pápago Well.
Standing water: San Cristóbal Wash, found but not used. (Thigh deep,
  100+ yards long.)

DAY 3, 31 MILES, PÁPAGO WELL
TO TULE WELL, AUGUST 24.

Water carried: 5 gallons each.
Water consumed: 4 gallons each.
Traveling time: 14 hours.
Hours traveled: 5:15 to 11:30 AM, 3:30 to 8:00 PM, and 9:30 PM to 1:00 AM.
Temperature Maximum: 104°F, with appalling humidity.

---

* All temperature maximums are based on Yuma, Arizona recordings; most stretches of the Camino del Diablo were considerably hotter.

Permanent water: Tule Well. (No longer water at Tule well.)
Standing water: On the Camino del Diablo, 100 yards west of Nameer's grave, found but not used (approximately 3 gallons).

DAY 4, 3 MILES, TULE WELL
TO TULE TANK, AUGUST 25.

Water carried: 5 gallons each.
Water consumed: 2 gallons each.
Traveling time: 1 hour.
Hours traveled: 5:00 to 6:00 PM (scheduled day off).
Temperature maximum: 106°F, with stifling humidity.
Seasonal water: Tule Tank, not used.
Standing water: None encountered.

DAY 5, 24 MILES, TULE TANK TO DAVIS PLAIN,
VIA JUAN BAUTISTA DE ANZA'S ROUTE FROM TINAJAS
ALTAS NORTH, AUGUST 26.

Water carried: 3 gallons each from Tule Tank to Tinajas Altas; 6 gallons each from Tinajas Altas north.
Water consumed: 5 gallons each (one while resting at Tinajas Altas).
Traveling time: 9 hours and 45 minutes.
Hours traveled: 5:30 to 11:30 AM and 5:15 to 9:00 PM.
Temperature maximum: 106°+F.
Permanent water: Tinajas Altas.
Standing water: None encountered, though there were indications water might be found at Coyote Water.

DAY 6, 32 MILES, JUAN BAUTISTA
DE ANZA'S ROUTE TO THE CAMINO DEL DIABLO
HISTORICAL MARKER.

Water carried: 5 gallons each.
Water consumed: 5 gallons each.
Traveling time: 11 hours and 45 minutes.
Hours traveled: 4:50 to 11:45 AM, and 4:45 to 9:30 PM.
Temperature maximum: 108°+F.

Permanent Water: Tinajas Altas.

Standing Water: None encountered, though there were indications water might be found in Spook Tank.

APPENDIX C

Desert Rescues

Supervisory Border Patrol Pilot Howard Aitken helped spearhead the rescue of sixteen illegal immigrants in the Tule Desert on August 28, 1998, (see entry #15 on page 175).

Despite the estimated four hundred to two thousand people who died of thirst on the Camino del Diablo in the 1800s, there were vague reports of many rescues among the thousands of immigrants and gold seekers who traversed the Road of the Devil during that period. However, until the U.S. Border Patrol began keeping official records in 1979, the actual number of rescues in the desert borderlands before then remains sketchy. In the years since, rescuers have reportedly saved the lives of 247 illegal immigrants in southwestern Arizona alone. What follows are some notable rescues in America's desert borderlands.

1. 1850s: Geographer Ronald L. Ives wrote that Pápagos living at Quitobaquito rescued many immigrants on the Camino del Diablo at great personal inconvenience and danger to themselves; Ives estimated these search and rescues numbered over a hundred after 1850.

2. 1855: Lt. N. Michler reported that a Mexican woman rescued three men she was traveling with across the Yuma Desert when she made a bold trek to Tinajas Altas and returned with a bota bag of water to save her dying companons.
   (Refer to Map V on pages 94 and 95.)

3. 1896: Capt. D.D. Gaillard of the International Boundary Commission reported that Don Pedro Aguirre of Buenos Aires, Arizona rescued seventeen men and one woman twenty-five miles east of Tinajas Altas by giving them water from his wagons.

4. 1905, August 23: Anthropologist W.J. McGee and Pápago tracker José nursed Pablo Valencia back to life at Tinajas Altas after he wandered the desert for six-and-a-half days without water.

5. 1917, January 27: The Ajo *Copper News* reported that a Capt. Greenway led two search teams on foot from Wellton, Arizona into Sonora's *Gran Desierto* to rescue two Army pilots who'd mistakingly landed in Mexico.

6. 1931, August: Ronald Ives reported that a Sonoyta, Sonora policeman rode horseback more than thirty miles in 120-degree heat to bring supplies to passengers stranded in a car wreck west of Agua Dulce.

7. 1941, August 6: Itinerant peddler Francisco Arvallo rescued 23 year old Francisco Flores and 19 year old Socorro Cornejo when their family's truck got stuck in the sand seventeen miles east of San Luís Río Colorado, Sonora. Seven other Cornejo family members and companions, who'd been without water for at least four days, died of thirst.

8. 1980, July 4-5: Fourteen Salvadorans were rescued in Organ Pipe Cactus National Monument by Border Patrol trackers and U.S.

Customs agents; thirteen people of the original party of thirty-one perished, two were never found, and one coyote escaped.

9. 1981, July 9: Twelve Mexican nationals were rescued by Border Patrol trackers in the Lechuguilla Desert south of Baker Peaks; one person from the original party of thirteen died.

10. 1985, June 16: Two Salvadorans were rescued by Border Patrol trackers in the San Cristóbal Valley; five of the original party of seven, which included three children, perished.

11. 1987, July 1: Twenty-two Mexican nationals from the state of Sinaloa were rescued in the San Cristóbal Valley south of Dateland by a three-man Marine helicopter crew, and thirty-two Border Patrol agents; three of the original party of twenty-five perished.

12. 1988, June 5: Thirty-one Mexican nationals from the state of Oaxaca were rescued by Border Patrol agents in the Sonoran desert northwest of Tucson; there are conflicting reports in Phoenix and Tucson newspapers whether this was a rescue or apprehension (off map).

13. 1996, February 29: Two men were rescued by Border Patrol trackers in the Tule Desert; the rescue is remarkable for the fact it was a winter rescue.

14. 1998, August: 113 illegal immigrants were rescued by Border Patrol agents in Sierra Blanca, Texas who found them suffocating in a tractor trailer rig 90 miles southeast of El Paso (off map).

15. 1998, August 28: A pilot for the U.S. Fish and Wildlife Service, Border Patrol trackers and pilots rescue 16 Mexican nationals from Guadalajara, Jalisco after their ruthless Mexican *coyote* abandoned them to die without water north of Tule Well (see photo page 126).

 * Many Border Patrol rescues, such as the August 28, 1998 rescue capsulized above, have gone unreported in the press.

** In 1990, the U.S. Border Patrol began a public ralations campaign in Mexico called "Say Out, Stay Alive" to discourage illegal immigrants from crossing the border.

BIBLIOGRAPHY

A headless raven lies on the bottom of José Juan Tank, a dry waterhole in the Barry M. Goldwater Range.

BOOKS

Abbey, Edward. *Cactus Country.* (Photographs by David Cavagnaro and Wolf Von Dem Bussche.) Alexandria, Virginia: Time-Life Books, 1973.

Allard, William Albert. *The Photographic Essay.* (Photographs by the author.) Boston: Bulfinch Press, 1989.

Annerino, John. *High Risk Photography: The Adventure Behind the Image.* (Photographs by the author.) Helena, Mont: American & World Geographic Publishing, 1991.

———. *Adventuring in Arizona.* San Francisco: Sierra Club Books, 1991a. (Revised edition 1996).

———. *Canyons of the Southwest: A Tour of the Great Canyon Country from Colorado to Northern Mexico.* (Photographs by the author.) San Francisco: Sierra Club Books, 1993.

———. *The Wild Country of Mexico: La tierra salvaje de México.* (Photographs by the author.) San Francisco: Sierra Club Books, 1994.

————. *People of Legend: Native Americans of the Southwest.* (Photographs by the author.) San Francisco: Sierra Club Books, 1996.

————. *Running Wild: An Extraordinary Adventure of the Human Spirit.* (Photographs by Christine Keith.) New York: Thunder's Mouth Press, 1997.

Ashabranner, Brent. *The Vanishing Border: A Photographic Journey Along Our Frontier with Mexico.* (Photographs by Paul Conklin.) New York: Dodd, Mead & Company, 1987.

Astorga-Almanza, Luís Alejandro. *Mitologia del "Narcotraficante" en México,* [Mythology of Drug Traffickers in Mexico]. México, D.F.: Universidad Nacional Autónoma de México, Plaza y Valdés, S.A. de C.V., 1995.

Barnes, William C. *Arizona Place Names.* (Revised and Enlarged by Byrd H. Granger.) Tucson: University of Arizona Press, 1985.

Bolton, Herbert Eugene. *Spanish Exploration in the Southwest: 1542-1706.* New York: Charles Scribner's Sons, 1916.

————. *Anza's California Expeditions.* Berkeley: University of California Press, 1930.

————. *Rim of Christendom: A Biography of Eusebio Francisco Kino, Pacific Coast Pioneer.* New York: Macmillan, 1936.

————. *Kino's Historical Memoir of Pimeria Alta.* 2 vols. Berkeley: University of California Press, 1948.

Brown, David E. *The Grizzly in the Southwest: Documentary of an Extinction.* Norman: University of Oklahoma Press, 1985.

Canfield, D. Lincoln. *The University of Chicago Spanish Dictionary,* 4th edition. Chicago: University of Chicago, 1978.

Carmony, Neil B., ed. *The Civil War in Apacheland: Sergeant George Hand's Diary: California, Arizona, West Texas, New Mexico, 1861-1864.* Silver City, NM: High Lonesome Books, 1996.

Carmony, Neil B., and David E. Brown, eds. *The Wilderness of the Southwest: Charles Sheldon's Quest for Desert Bighorn Sheep and Adventures with the Havasupai and Seri Indians.* (Photographs by Charles Sheldon and others.) Salt Lake City: University of Utah Press, 1994.

Conover, Ted. *Coyotes: A Journey Through the Secret World of America's Illegal Aliens.* New York: Vintage Departures, 1987.

Coues, Elliott, ed. *On the Trail of a Spanish Pioneer: The Diary and Itinerary of Francisco Garcés in His Travels through Sonora, Arizona, and California 1775-1776.* New York: F.P. Harper, 1900.

Crouch, Brodie, *Jornada del Muerto: A Pageant of the Desert.* Spokane, Washington: Arthur H. Clark Co., 1989.

Ezell, Paul. "The Areneños (Sand Pápago)—Interview with Alberto Celaya" in *Spanish Borderlands Sourcebooks: Ethnology of Northwest Mexico,* 6. New York: Garland Publishing, 1992.

Fletcher, Colin. *The Thousand Mile Summer: In Desert and High Sierra.* Berkeley: Howell–North Books, 1964.

Forbes, Robert Humphrey, *Crabb's fillibustering Expedition into Sonora, 1857.* Tucson: Arizona Silhouettes, 1952.

Friar, John G., and George W. Kelly. *A Practical Spanish Grammar For Border Patrol Officers.* Washington, DC: U.S. Department of Justice, Immigration and Naturalization Service, 1972.

Galván, Roberto A., and Richard V. Teschner. *El Diccionario del Español Chicano/ The Dictionary of Chicano Spanish.* Chicago: National Textbook Co., 1992.

Gray, Andrew B. *Survey of a Route for the Southern Pacific Railroad on the 32nd Parallel, for the Texas Western Railroad Co.* Cincinnati: Wrightson and Co., 1856.

Haley, J. Evetts. *Jeff Milton, A Good Man with a Gun.* Norman: University of Oklahoma Press, 1948.

Hall, Douglas Kent. *Border: Life on the Line.* (Photographs by the author.) New York: Abbeville Press, 1988.

Hallenbeck, Cleve, and Juanita A. Williams. *Legends of the Spanish Southwest.* Glendale, CA: Arthur H. Clark, Co, 1938.

Hartmann, William K. *Desert Heart: Chronicles of the Sonoran Desert.* (Photographs by the author.) Tucson: Fisher Books, 1989.

Horgan, Paul, *Great River: The Río Grande in North American History.* 2 volumes. New York: Rinehart and Company, 1954.

Hornaday, William T. *Campfires on Desert and Lava.* (Photographs by John M. Phillips and others.) New York: Charles Scribner's Sons, 1908.

Ives, Ronald L. *Land of Lava, Ash, and Sand: The Pinacate Region of Northwestern Mexico.* Tucson: Arizona Historical Society, 1989.

James, George Wharton, *The Wonders of the Colorado Desert (Southern California): Its Rivers and its Mountains, its Canyons and its Springs, its Life and its History, Pictured and Described.* (Photographs by the author, pen and ink sketches by Carl Eytel.) Volume I. Boston: Little, Brown, and Company, 1906.

Langewiesche, William. *Cutting for Sign.* New York: Pantheon, 1993.

Lumholtz, Carl. *New Trails in Mexico: An Account of One Year's Exploration in Northwestern Sonora, Mexico, and Southwestern Arizona 1909–1910.* (Photographs by the author.) New York: Charles Scribner's Sons, 1912.

Manje, Juan Mateo. *Luz de Tierra Incógnita: Unknown Arizona and Sonora, 1693–1721.* (Translation and photographs by Harry J. Karns, maps by Don Bufkin.) Tucson: Arizona Silhouettes, 1954.

Oden, Peter. *The Desert Trackers: Men of the Border Patrol.* Yuma, AZ: Peter Oden, 1975.

Ortiz, Alfonso, ed. *Handbook of North American Indians: Southwest.* Vol. 10. Washington, DC.: Smithsonian Institution, 1983.

Perkins, Clifford Alan. *Border Patrol: With the U.S. Immigration Service on the*

Mexican Boundary 1910–1954. (Photographs by W.D. Smithers.) El Paso: Texas Western Press, 1978.

Poppa, Terrence E. *Drug Lord: The Life and Death of a Mexican Kingpin.* New York: Pharos Books, 1990.

Pumpelly, Raphael. *Across America and Asia: Notes of Five Years' Journey Around the World and of Residence in Arizona, Japan, and China.* New York: Leypoldt and Holt, 1870.

Rak, Mary Kidder. *Border Patrol.* Boston: Houghton, Mifflin, Co., 1938.

Roosevelt, Kermit. *The Happy Hunting-Grounds.* New York: Charles Scribner's Sons, 1920.

Shannon, Elaine. *Desperados: Latin Drug Lords, U.S. Lawmen, and the War America Can't Win.* New York: Penguin Books, 1988.

Spilken, Aaron. *Escape.* New York: New American Library, 1983.

Smith, Olga Wright. *Gold On the Desert.* Albuquerque: University of New Mexico Press, 1956.

Sykes, Godfrey. *A Westerly Trend.* Tucson: Arizona Pioneers' Historical Society, 1944.

Thomas, Robert K. "Pápago Land Use: West of the Pápago Indian Reservation South of the Gila River and the Problems of Sand Pápago Identity" in *Spanish Borderlands Sourcebooks: Ethnology of Northwest Mexico, 6.* New York: Garland Publishing, 1992.

Tyler, Ronnie C. *The Big Bend: A History of the Last Texas Frontier.* Washington, DC: U.S. Department of the Interior, 1975.

Velasco, José Francisco. *Noticias Estadísticas del Estado de Sonora.* Hermosillo: Gobierno del Estado de Sonora, 1985.

Walker, Henry P., and Donald Bufkin. *Historical Atlas of Arizona.* Norman: University of Oklahoma Press, 1978.

Wambaugh, Joseph. *Lines and Shadows.* New York: Bantam Books, 1984.

Weisman, Alan. *La Frontera: The United States Border With Mexico.* (photographs by Jay Dusard.) New York: Harcourt Brace Jovanovich, 1986.

HUMAN RIGHTS REPORTS

Cavallaro, James L., and Allyson Collins. "United States, Frontier Injustice: Human Rights Abuses Along the U.S. Border with Mexico Persist Amid Climate of Impunity." Human Rights Watch/Americas. 5:4 (May 13, 1993): 1–46.

Collins, Allyson, and Lee Tucker. "United States, Crossing the Line: Human Rights Abuses Along the U.S. Border Persist Amid Climate of Impunity." Human Rights Watch/Americas. 7:4. (April 1995): 1–37.

Lutz, Ellen L. *Human Rights in Mexico: A Policy of Impunity.* An America's Watch Report. New York: Human Rights Watch, 1990.

Roberson, Tod. "Mexico Denounced as Anti-Migrant: U.S.-Bound Itinerants Complain of Beatings, Rape While in Jail." Washington Post. December 20, 1994: A-1 and A-32.

Solis, Dianne. "Mexico Has Its Own Border 'Nightmare': Police Beatings in the U.S. are Mirrored in Tales of Central Americans." The Wall Street Journal. May 1, 1996: A-11.

JOURNALS, MAGAZINES, AND REPORTS

Annerino, John. "Heroic Trackers." (Photo essay by the author/Gamma-Liaison). Police, vol. 12, no. 3 (March 1988): 29–33.

———. "Rescue-1." (Photo essay by the author/Gamma-Liaison). Proceedings, U.S. Naval Institute, vol.115/9/1039 (September 1989): 57–59.

———. "Path of Fire." (Photo essay by the author). Phoenix, vol. 26, no. 9 (September 1991): 106–117.

———. "Hunger in Paradise, Tarahumara babies wither, die from starvation." (Photographs by the author). The Arizona Republic, Perspective, E 1–2, January 22, 1995.

———. " Viva Zapata! Mexico's forgotten poor crippled by peso crisis." (Photographs by the author). The Arizona Republic, Perspective, E 1–2, March 12, 1995.

———. "Mexico on the Edge, El Fantasma and others in the middle class caught in financial crash, Barzonistas battle corrupt banks, financial disasters." (Photograph by the author). The Arizona Republic, Perspective, H 1–2, March 10, 1996.

———. "Displaced and Desperate, Crash of peso drives Indians off land, into streets, Displaced Indians fill streets of the damned." (Photograph by the author). The Arizona Republic, Perspective, H 1–2, March 24, 1996.

———. "Behind the Lines, Ageless Agent Gathers Inside Dope Among Bloody Betrayals, Agent Survives 40-year Drug War Inside Mexico." (Photograph by the author.) The Arizona Republic, Perspective, H-1-2, May 19, 1996.

Barney, James M. "El Camino del Diablo." Arizona Highways Magazine. Vol. 19, No. 3 (March 1943): 14–19.

Brickler, Stanley K. et al. Natural Resource Management Plan for Luke Air Force Range. Tucson: University of Arizona, 1986.

Broyles, Bill. "Desert Thirst: The Ordeal of Pablo Valencia." Journal of Arizona History. 23:4 (Winter 1982): 357–380.

Broyles, Bill, Richard Felger, et al. "Our Grand Desert: A Gazetteer for Northwester Sonora, Southwestern Arizona, and Northeastern Baja California," in Dry Borders, Journal of the Southwest, vol. 39, nos. 3 and 4, (Autumn-Winter 1997): 703–856.

Broyles, Bill, Tom Harlan, et al. "W.J. McGee's Desert Thirst as Disease." Journal of the Southwest vol. 30, no. 2. (Summer 1988): 222–227.

Childs, Thomas. "History of an Old-Timer." (Letter to the Editor.) Desert Magazine. 12:12 (October 1949):27.

Childs, Thomas, as written to Henry F. Dobyns. "A Sketch of the Sand Indians." The Kiva. 19:2–4 (Spring 1954): 27–39.

Crampton, John F. "Mohawk Station—Early Days." Unpublished paper on file at the Arizona Historical Society, Tucson, nd.

Dedera, Don. "Sylvester: Remains to be Seen." Arizona Highways, vol. 59, no. 10 (October 1983): 40.

Erbeck, Willard W. "Death on the Desert . . . " (Letter to the Editor.) Desert Magazine. 27:12 (December 1964): 42.

Gaillard, Capt. David DuBose. "The Perils and Wonders of a True Desert." Cosmopolitan. Vol 21 (October 1896): 592–605.

Green, Jerome A. *Historic Resource Study: Organ Pipe Cactus National Monument.* Denver: U.S. Department of Interior, 1977.

Hammer, Joshua. "Death in the Desert." (Photograph by Adam Harju.) Newsweek, (August 24, 1988): 29

Hoy, Bill, "Hardscrabble Days at the Ajo Mines: George Kippen's Diary, 1855–1858." Journal of Arizona History, 36 (1995): 233–250.

———. "The George Kippen Diary." Unpublished notes, 1–26, nd.

Ives, Ronald L. "The Sonoran Railroad Project." The Journal of Geography. Vol. XLVIII, No. 5 (May 1949): 197–206.

Kippen, George. *Arizona Mines, Gadsden Purchase, George Kippen.* (Handwritten diary.) Phoenix: Arizona State Museum, 1854.

Mason, William. "The Sonora Trail." Terra. (Summer 1963): 10–13. Los Angeles County Museum.

McGee, W.J. "The Old Yuma Trail." National Geographic Magazine. Vol. 12 (March–April 1901): 103–143.

McGee, W.J. "Desert Thirst as Disease." Interstate Medical Journal. 13:3 (March 1906): 279–300.

Michler, Lt. N. "Report of Lieut. Michler" in *United States and Mexico Boundary Survey* by W.H. Emory. Washington, D.C.: U.S. Government Printing Office, 1857.

Nichol, A.A. "O'Neill's Grave in O'Neill's Pass in the O'Neill Mountains." Random Papers, Southwestern National Monuments. (July 1939): 65–67.

Rodríguez, Nestor. "Death at the Border," College of Social Sciences, Center for Immigration Research, University of Houston, 1997.

Sharp, Jay W. "Jornada del Muerto." New Mexico Magazine. Vol. 63, No. 1 (January 1985): 18–20.

Van Valkenburgh, Richard. "Tom Childs of Ten-Mile Wash." Desert Magazine. 9:2 (December 1945): 3–6.

Zink, Orion. "Mystery Death in the Dunes." Desert Magazine. Vol. 12, No. 4 (February 1949): 11–15.

WATER-SUPPLY PAPERS

Brown, Bryan T., and R. Roy Johnson. "The Distribution of Bedrock Depressions (Tinajas) as Sources of Surface Water in Organ Pipe Cactus National Monument, Arizona." Journal of the Arizona-Nevada Academy of Science. 18:2 (1983): 61–68.

Broyles, Bill. "Surface Water Resources for Prehistoric Peoples in Western Paguería of the North American Southwest." Journal of Arid Environments. Vol. 33 (1996): 483–495.

Bryan, Kirk. "Origin of Rock Tanks and Charcos." American Journal of Science. Vol. 50 (1920): 188–206.

———. "Routes to Desert Watering Places in Pápago Country, Arizona." U.S. Geological Survey Water-Supply Paper 490-D: (1922): 317–429. U.S. Government Printing Office, Washington, D.C.

———. "The Pápago Country, Arizona." U.S. Geological Survey Water-Supply Paper 499, U.S. Government Printing Office, Washington, DC, 436 pp. 1925.

Ives, Ronald L. "Kiss Tanks." Weather. Vol. 42.(1962):194–196.

Ross, Clyde P. "The Lower Gila Region, Arizona: A Geographic, Geologic, and Hydrologic Reconnaissance with a Guide to Desert Watering Places." U.S. Geological Survey Water-Supply Paper 498, U.S. Government Printing Office, Washington, DC, 237pp. 1923.

NEWSPAPER ARTICLES AND REPORTS

(Listed by Date)

1941, August 6: "Seven Perish On Blistering Desert Road, Two Survive Ordeal of Thirst, Heat As Truck Stalls." The Arizona Republic: A-1. Associated Press.

1974, May 29: "Thirst, heat kill 4 at gunnery range; 5th feared dead." The Arizona Republic: A-1, A-8. Anonymous.

1974, May 30: "Survivors recount fatal ordeal on desert." The Arizona Republic: B-1. Dave Spriggs.

1974, May 31: "5th shell-hunter's body found near road on gunnery range." The Arizona Republic: A-26. Gordon Robbins.

1977, March 1: State of Arizona, Appellee, v. Louis J. Dykes Appellant. No. 1 CA-CR 905. Court of Appeals of Arizona, Division 1, Department C. Phoenix.

1980, July 6: "2 aliens found dead in desert; 7 others saved." The Arizona Republic: A-1. Anonymous.

1980, July 7: "Eleven more bodies of illegal aliens found in desert." The Arizona Republic: A-1, A-2. Randy Collier. (Photographs by Michael Ging.)

1980, July 7: "'We wiped our faces with (urine) . . . we were so thirsty'." The Arizona Republic: A-1, A-2. Anonymous.

1980, July 7: "Illegal Aliens' Desert Horror—13 Found Dead." The San Francisco Chronicle: A-1. Anonymous.

1980, July 10: "4 Salvadoran desert victims may have been strangled." Tucson Citizen: 1-A, 7-A. Anonymous.

1980, July 10: "Her three daughters died in the desert." Tucson Citizen: 1-A. Louis Sahagun.

1980, July 21: "Death March in the Desert." Newsweek: 55. Dennis A. Williams with Martin Kasindorf. (Photograph by Michael Ging.)

1980, July 21: "Deathtrap, Thirteen aliens die in desert." Time: 22. Anonymous. (Photographs by Michael Ging.)

1980, July 21: "The sun above, the dead below." Macleans: 21. Arturo F. González.(Photographs by White-Gamma/Liaison and AP).

1981, July 10: "Border agents rescue 12 Mexicans in desert, 1 alien dies before group is located east of Yuma." The Arizona Republic: A-1. Bill Ahrens.

1981, July 11: "Smuggling ruled out in alien rescue." Arizona Daily Star: 12-A. Associated Press.

1981, July 11: "Never again, aliens vow after rescue." The Arizona Republic: A-1, A-27. Bill Ahrens.

1982, September 17: "Desert trek kills at least 3 Mexicans . . . 8 aliens missing, reports say." Arizona Daily Star: 1-A, 9-A. Ray Panzarella.

1982, September 18: "Border Patrol confirms finding 3 aliens' bodies." Arizona Daily Star: E-5. Ray Panzarella.

1982, October 27: "Real aliens were Geraldo and Co." Arizona Daily Star: 1-B. R.H. Ring.

1983, August 22: "The trek that can last for eternity." Tucson Citizen, (special report): 4 pp. Charles Bowden. (Photographs by P.K. Weis, Bill Broyles, John Hemmer.)

1985, June 18: "5 suspected aliens die in desert near Yuma." The Arizona Republic: B-1. Republic Staff/Associated Press.

1985, June 19: "Another Salvadoran from trek found alive." Arizona Daily Star: 1-B. Associated Press.

1985, September 12: "Union, bank to focus on 60 aliens' deaths." The Arizona Republic: A-2. Andy Hall.

1985, September 13: "Valley National to study ranch's link to aliens' deaths." The Arizona Republic: A-1, A-2. Andy Hall.

1985, September 27: "Deadly stretch of desert 'the place where the devil plays'." The Phoenix Gazette: A-2. Tony Natale.

1985, October 2. "Illegal aliens find haven in rest area after tiring, perilous trek across desert." The Phoenix Gazette: A-3, A-4. John Dougherty.

1985, October 6: "Illegal aliens take fatal gamble on Arizona desert." Chicago Tribune: 103: F13, E14. James Coates.

1985, December 4–10: "The Way to Whitewing,: Many of those caught by the Border Patrol admit to heading toward Whitewing. Many of them also report sighting bodies and bones along the way." New Times: 18, 19, 24, 26, 28, 30, 32, 33. Doug MacEachern and Rubén Hernández.

1986, February 19: "Records show desert deaths linked to VNB ranch." The Phoenix Gazette: F-1. John Dougherty.

1986, May 6: "Team formed to halt alien deaths in desert corridor: 3 squads will hunt for illegals missing along 50-mile swath." The Arizona Republic: B-2. Andy Hall.

1986, May 7–13: "Troubled Waters: Illegal immigrants are swimming our borders . . . and dying there." New Times: 24–25,32,35,37. Doug MacEachern and Rubén Hernández. (Photographs by Doug MacEachern.)

1986, August 3: "Path of Fire: Aliens' desert route from Mexico to U.S. is one of sun, thirst, anguish—and death." The Arizona Republic: A-1, A-11. Andy Hall. (Photographs by Tom Story.)

1986, August 3: "Probe fails to prove ranch illegally enticed Mexicans." The Arizona Republic: A-1, A-11. Andy Hall.

1986, September 21: "Death march across desert: Aliens risk it all for US jobs." Sacramento Bee: A-1, A-28. Chris Bowman.

1986, September 21: "Canal a savior, a killer: Sight of floating corpses is commonplace." Sacramento Bee: A-28. Chris Bowman. (Photographs by Sandy Engebretsen.)

1986, September 29: "Pursuers become desert rescuers." Tucson Citizen: 91:F8,E9. Tom Childs.

1986, n.d.: "Hunt for Better Life Leads Aliens to 'Season of Death." Los Angeles Times: A-1, A-12. Bill Curry.

1987, June 20: "Desert Crossing hazardous duty for illegal aliens." Arizona Daily Star: 1-B. Kathy Scott.

1987, July 15: "3 Aliens Die, 22 Rescued East of Yuma: Drank urine and ate toothpaste, 1 says." The Arizona Republic: A-1, A-2. Gene Varn and Butch Cardeñas.

1987, July 15: "Job search ends in death, tragedy." Yuma Daily Sun:A-1, A-2. John Vaughn.

1987, July 17: "Deaths touch foe of illegal aliens." USA Today: 2-A. Anonymous. (Photograph by KPNX-TV, Phoenix.)

1987, July 19: "The Trek: Border Patrol turns savior." Arizona Daily Star: 125:A13. Mark Holman Turner.

1987, July 29: "Heavy toll hasn't deterred aliens from trying to cross desert." Dallas Morning News: 125:A1. David L. Marcus.

1987, August 14: "2 Mexicans are indicted in alien-smuggling case." The Arizona Republic: B-3. Andy Hall.

1988, May 9: "Decomposed." Yuma Daily Sun: A-2. Anonymous.

1988, June 5: "36 aliens found in desert near Tucson: Group checked at hospital; OK but dehydrated." The Arizona Republic: B-1, B-9. Sam Negri and Dee Ralles.

1988, June 5: "Desert treks turned deadly for other aliens." Arizona Daily Star: A-4. Chris Limberis.

1988, June 6: "Rescued aliens torn by hopes: 'Dollar dream' eludes workers." The Arizona Republic: A-1, A-6. Jerry Kramer. (Photographs by Linda Seeger.)

1989, June 18: "Tinajas Altas: Life hid in the stones." The Arizona Republic: T-3. Bob Thomas.

1989, July 14: "Pilot dies in crash of border airplane." Yuma Daily Sun: A-1. Tony Carroll. (Photograph by Beth Bidne.)

1989, July 15: "Probe begun in crash that killed agent." Yuma Daily Sun: A-1, A-9. Loren Listiak.

1989, July 16: "Border Patrolman called quiet hero who saved lives." Yuma Daily Sun: A-1. T.M. Shultz.

1989, November 6: "Border game goes over the edge to twist human tragedy into fun." The Arizona Republic: 1N5. Julie Labaco.

1990, July 6: "Apparent illegal alien found dead in desert." Yuma Daily Sun: 3. Anonymous.

1990, October 13: "Mexican boy lost a month dies alone." Tucson Citizen: 1-A, 3-A. Rubén Hernández.

1991, July 16: "Illegal alien found dead in desert after trek from border." Arizona Daily Star: 1-A. Joe Salkowski.

1991, July 17: "Illegal alien left behind by smuggler dies in heat: wife survives, seeks to send body home." The Arizona Republic: B-1. Keith Rosenblum.

1991, August 16: "Tourists discover body: Organ Pipe heat may have killed illegal immigrant." Tucson Citizen: 1-A. David L. Teibel.

1991, August 17: "Illegal alien dies in desert south of Ajo." Arizona Daily Star: 1-A, 4-A. Donnie S. Henshaw.

1991, August 25: "Aliens with dreams of better life in U.S. face pitiless desert." The Arizona Republic: A-1. Paul Brinkley-Rogers. (Photographs by Mary Annette Pember.)

1991, August 25: "Widow tells of fatal trek across desert." The Arizona Republic: A-17. Keith Rosenblum.

1992, June 4: "Luke pilot killed in crash of jet fighter near Gila Bend." The Arizona Republic: B-2. Anonymous.

1993, June 20: "Heat-related death of alien crossing desert is first since '91; woman found near Mexican border." The Arizona Republic: B-1. Chuck Kelly.

1993, July 9: "Rain may hurt search for Guatemalens: Illegal immigrant dead, 8 lost in desert." Phoenix Gazette: A-1. Victor Dricks and The Associated Press.

1993, July 10: "Search called off for Guatemalans missing in desert; 8 aliens feared dead, but others are caught." The Arizona Republic: A-1. David Fritze and The Associated Press. (Photographs by Charles Krejcsi.)

1993, July 10: "Survival Test: To those who make it, trek through desert is worth the danger." Phoenix Gazette: A-1, A-2. Roberto Sánchez. (Photograph by Michael Chow.)

1993, July 10: "They couldn't carry enough water, experts say." The Arizona Republic: A-2. David Canella.

1993, July 12: "Harsh desert often only road for immigrants; possibility of better life in U.S. makes risky trek worthwhile." Phoenix Gazette: A-1. Russ Hemphill and Betty Reid. (Photograph by Randy Reid.)

1993, October 9: "2 found dead in desert: Deputies believe the unidentified men may be illegal immigrants who died of exposure." Tucson Citizen: 1-A. Angela Rábago-Mussi.

1993, October 12: "Dead men tried to light signal fire." Tucson Citizen: C-1. Anonymous.

1993, December 4: "A 21-year-old Mexican national who entered the United States illegally but apparently was on his way home was found dead . . . " The Arizona Republic: B-2. Anonymous.

1994, June 25: "Desert search on for illegal immigrants; 110-degree heat poses danger to 18 Guatemalans." The Arizona Republic: B-1. The Associated Press and Richard F. Casey.

1995, September 5: "Desert as deadly as it ever was statistics keep reminding us." The Arizona Republic: A-1. Charles Kelly. (Photograph by Michael Ging.)

1995, November 8: "Survivor tells grim tale of pal's death in desert." Arizona Daily Star: 12-A. Associated Press.

1996, May 4: "Border Patrol saves 13 in desert." Tucson Citizen: 1-A. Pamela Hartman.

1996, May 17: "Heat may have killed woman found in desert near Douglas." Arizona Daily Star: A-1. Ignacio Ibarra.

1996, May 21: "Peruvian woman met death in heat of desert crossing." Arizona Daily Star: 1-B. Ignacio Ibarra.

1996, June 16: "Bodies of missing illegals found." The Arizona Republic: B-4. Associated Press.

1996, June 17: "Border Patrol discovers bodies of 2 more Mexican nationals." The Arizona Republic: B-2. Associated Press.

1996, June 18: "Dying for a Dream: Illegal immigrants risk and lose lives in sizzling desert." The Arizona Repulic: A-1, A-6. Mark Shaffer. (Photographs by Rob Schumacher and Randy Reid.)

1996, June 20: "Survivor recounts fatal border cross." The Arizona Republic: B-1,B-2. Marina Dobrosavljevic.

1996, June 22: "Illegal immigrant's body found in Arizona Desert: Victim is 7th this week; officials fear there's an 8th." The Arizona Republic: A-20 and B-1. Mark Shaffer.

1996, July 4: "Remains of 3 suspected illegals discovered." Arizona Daily Star: 1-A, 14-A. Ignacio Ibarra.

1996, July 28: *Where Dreams Die*, (1st in five-part Perspective series.) "Devil's Road tortures those who cross its path." The Arizona Republic: H-1–3. Photographs, text, sidebars, and map by John Annerino.

1996, August 11: *Where Dreams Die*, (2nd in Perspective series.) "Left Behind: Day-to-day despair haunts families of Old Mexico." The Arizona Republic: H-1–2. Photographs and text by John Annerino.

1996, August 25: *Where Dreams Die*, (3rd in Perspective series.) "Deadly Walk of Life: Desperate Mexican's cross Arizona's Killing ground." The Arizona Republic: H-1–2. Photographs, text, and map by John Annerino.

1996, September 8: *Where Dreams Die*, (4th in Perspective series.) "John Doe Mexican: Arizona's deserts have claimed hundreds—many are nameless." The Arizona Republic: H-1–2. Photographs, text, memoriam, and map by John Annerino.

1996, September 22" *Where Dreams Die*, (last in Perspective series.) "Sweating it Out: Invisible migrants pin hopes on hard work." Photographs and text by John Annerino.

1996, October 3. "Migrant series was moving." (Letter to the Editor.) The Arizona Republic: B-6. Diane Kennedy Pike.

1997, May 27: "Howitzer shell found." "Missing man sought." Yuma Daily Sun: 3. Anonymous.

1997, May 29: "She was taken far too soon." Tucson Citizen:2-A. Paul L. Allen.

1997, July 2: "Body found after brush fire doused." Yuma Daily Sun: 3. Anonymous.

1997, July 3: "Mexican man dies trying to cross desert." Arizona Daily Star: 1-B. Hipolito R. Corella.

1997, July 8: "Apparent illegal entrant dies near Douglas." Arizona Daily Star: 2-B. Anonymous.

1997, July 19: "24 live through desert journey: Border Patrol agents save illegal immigrants lost near Sells without water, in searing heat." Tucson Citizen: B-2. Larry Copenhaver.

1997, August 7: "6 from Mexico drown in ditch." The Arizona Republic: A-1, A-19. Mark Shaffer. (Photograph by Jeffrey Scott.)

1997, August 12: "Illegals take fatal risks: Death toll along border at 'epidemic levels." The Arizona Republic: A-1, A-2. Mark Shaffer.

1997, August 17: "A cruel crossing: 2 Mexicans sought work, but found death." Arizona Daily Star: 1-A, 8–9-A. Tim Steller. (Photographs by Jeffrey Scott.)

1997, August 27: "Last two bodies in Douglas drowning returning to Mexico." Arizona Daily Star: 1-B. Ignacio Ibarra.

1997, September 7: "New 'gate' doesn't deter immigrants, just reroutes them." The Arizona Republic: A-16. Dana Calvo, AP.

1998, April 13: The border's big easy: Task force protects illegals from predators." Arizona Daily Star: 1-A, 7-A, 8-A. Ignacio Ibarra. (Photographs by Jeffrey Scott.)

1998, May 31: "'Going through tremendous growth"; Border Patrol recruiting skyrockets." The Arizona Republic: A-29. Nancy San Martín, Dallas Morning News.

1998, July 2: "Illegal entrant dies after crossing border." Arizona Daily Star: 2-B. Tim Steller.

1998, July 16: "Immigrants after water break into Ariz. church, Border Patrol worries as heat drags on." Arizona Daily Star: 1-B, 3-B. Monica Mendoza.

1998, July 19: "3rd day of searching fails to turn up missing cowboy." Arizona Daily Star. Tom Colins.

1998, July 28: "2 more die on border in searing desert heat." Tucson Citizen: 1-A, 6-A. Pamela Hartman.

1998, July 28: "Woman dies in familiar desert drama, Fellow illegals ignore guide and give aid, but it's too late." Arizona Daily Star: 1-A, 3-A. Inger Sandal.

1998, July 30: "Illegal crosser 4th to die from heat in a week, Deputies find the body of a man near Avra Valley after receiving a call from his group." Tucson Citizen: 1-C, 4-C. Pamela Hartman and Patrick Revere.

1998, July 31: "Agents search desert to rescue lost illegal alien, but hope fades." Arizona Daily Star: 2-B. Tim Steller.

1998, August 14: "'It's an endless land', Monsoon season can spell difference between life, death." Arizona Daily Star: 1-A, 6-A. Tim Steller. (Photographs by Bruce McClelland.)

1998, August 21: "Mexico City woman is 9th to die after illegally crossing into Arizona." Arizona Daily Star: 1-B. Ignacio Ibarra.

1998, August 24: "Help too late for 1 of 6 crossing desert." Arizona Daily Star: 2-B. L. Anne Newell.

1998, August 26: "113 illegals saved from sweltering rig." Arizona Daily Star: 11-A. Associated Press.

1998, September 15: "Border Patrol rescues 100th entrant; condition is critical." Arizona Daily Star: 3-B. Ignacio Ibarra.

1998, October 13: "Train kills 6 men sleeping on tracks." Arizona Republic: A-4. Associated Press.

1999, January 12: "1,000 a day caught at border." Tucson Citizen: 1-A. Pamela Hartman.

1999, January 28: "Illegal immigrant describes wounding by Patagonia man; 'There was no reason for him to shoot at us.'" Tucson Citizen: 1-A, 4-A. Pamela Hartman. (Photograph by Gary Gaynor.)

1999, February 6: "Clinton budget axes Border Patrol hires." Arizona Republic: A-29. Jessica Wehrmann, Scripps Howard.

INCIDENT REPORTS, LETTERS, AND INTERVIEWS

(Listed by Date)

n.d: Desert Death File List: beginning with 7/11/82 (Case#: P-6014-82) and ending with 10/20/85 (Case#:Y854285). Anonymous.

1982, July 11: YCSD Incident Report, Case#: R-6014-82. Victim: C. Juan Ceja Contreras.

1982, August 2: YCSD Incident Report, Case#: R-6525-82. Victim: Unknown, one human skull with three teeth found.

1982, August 20: YCSD Incident Report, Case#: R-7285-82. Victims: Luís Guillen González, José Rosendo Ramírez, and Carlos Vásquez Esparza.

1982, September 3: YCSD Incident Report, Case#: R-7392-82. Victim: José León Beltrán.

1982, September 10: YCSD Incident Report, Case#: R-7673-82. Victim: Tomás Torres Vargas.

1982, September 18: YCSD Incident Report, Case#: R-7799-82. Victim: "John Doe Mexican."

1982, November 25: YCSD Incident Report, Case#: R-9579-82. Victim: Unknown, one human skull found.

1983, February 9: YCSD Incident Report, Case#: R-0862-83. Victim: Unknown, human bones found.

1983, April 13: YCSD Incident Report, Case#: R-2510-83. Victim: Unknown, leg bones and water jug found.

1983, May 29: YCSD Incident Report, Case#: R-3647-83. Victim: Efraín Bueno López.

1983, July 28: YCSD Incident Report, Case#: R-4888-83. Victim: Rosendo Gómez Vásquez.

1983, September 15: YCSD Incident Report, Case#: R-5987-83. Victim: "Mexican alien," body found.

1983, September 15: YCSD Incident Report, Case#: R-5994-83. Victim: Vicente Espinosa.

1983, October 21: YCSD Incident Report, Case#: R-6771-83. Victim: Unknown, six human bones found, one leg bone with pin.

1983, November 5: YCSD Incident Report, Case#: R-7097-83. Victim: Unknown, partial skull and leg bones found.

1983, November 6: YCSD Incident Report, Case#: R-7114-83. Victim: Unknown, mummified body found.

1983, November 9: YCSD Incident Report, Case#: R-7168-83. Victims: Cornelia Alvárez Vela and John Doe.

1984, June 3: YCSD Incident Report, Case#: Y-3886-84. Victims: Joaquín Piñeda Avila and John Doe.

1984, June 25: YCSD Incident Report, Case#: Y-4398-84. Victim: Francisco Avila-Herrera.

1984, September 7: YCSD Incident Report, Case#: Y-6342-84. Victim: Unknown, one human skull with brain matter found.

1984, September 17: YCSD Incident Report, Case#: Y-6592-84. Victim: Unknown, decomposed body found.

1984, November 5: YCSD Incident Report, Case#: Y-7944-84. Victim: Unknown, body and plastic water jug found.

1984, November 9: YCSD Incident Report, Case#: Y-8041-84. Victim: John Doe, decomposed body found.

1984, December 3: YCSD Incident Report, Case#: [illegible.] Victim: Unknown, human skull found.

1985, February 23: YCSD Incident Report, Case#: Y-1605-85. Victims: Unknown, remains of two bodies found.

1985, June 10: YCSD Incident Report, Case#: Y-5069-85. Victim: John Doe, body and four water jugs found.

1985, June 16: YCSD Incident Report, Case#: Y-5207-85. Victims: Rosario Soriano de Martínez, Luís Edgardo Martínez, Carlos Adalberto Martínez, and Dora Alicia Meña. ["Betti Jane Doe" not found].

1985, July 18: YCSD Incident Report, Case#: Y-6038-85. Victim: "John Doe Mexican," body and plastic jug of urine found.

1985, July 23: YCSD Incident Report, Case#: Y-6186-85. Victim: Arturo Castillo Ortega.

1985, n.d. Calendar of Events at the Whitewing Ranch, beginning July 29, 1985 and ending September 30, 1985. Anonymous.

1985, July 30: YCSD Incident Report, Case#: Y-6363-85. Victim: Miguel Ruíz Juárez.

1985, August 8: YCSD Incident Report, Case#: Y-6622-85. Victim: José Luís Casteñada-Mendoza.

1985, August 29: YCSD Incident Report, Case#: Y-7155-85. Victims: Rafaél Zamora and "John Doe Mexican."

1985, September 1: YCSD Incident Report, Case#: Y-7282-85. Victim: Unknown, Mexican male.

1985, September 8: YCSD Incident Report, Case#: Y-7466-85. Victim: Unknown, human skull and jawbone found.

1985, September 12: YCSD Incident Report, Case#: Y-7568-85. Victim: Ramón Flores López.

1985, September 14: YCSD Incident Report, Case#: Y-7610-85. Victim: José Angel Sotelo-Muñoz.

1985, October 20: YCSD Incident Report, Case#: Y-8542-85. Victim: Unknown, body found.

1985, December 9: YCSD Incident Report, Case#: Y-10219-85. Victim: Unknown, skull found.

1985, December 29: YCSD Incident Report, Case#: Y-11004-85. Victim: Unknown, skull and bones found.

1986, March 10: Letter from Austin L. Carroll, Corporal, Yuma County Sheriff Department to Maricopa County Organizing Project regarding Desert Deceased, Case #'s: Y-11004-85, and Y-10219-85.

1986, May 1: Signed statement by Carlos Cobarubia Mesa regarding discovery of three unidentified bodies while crossing the desert borderlands between April 21 and April 22, 1986.

1986, June 5: YCSD Incident Report, Case#: Y-6592-86. Victim: "John Doe Mexican," body found.

1986, June 9: YCSD Incident Report, Case#: Y-6742-86. Victim: "John Doe Mexican," body found.

1986, June 9: YCSD Incident Report, Case#: Y-6744-86. Victim: "John Doe Mexican," body found.

1986, June 25–26: Desert Death File from Robert J. Mellet regarding the death in the desert of Roberto Miranda Ramírez.

1986, July 24: YCSD Incident Report, Case#: Y-8774-86. Victim: Unknown, lower jawbone and other bones found.

1986, July 29: YCSD Incident Report, Case#: Y-9012-86. Victim: Unknown, body found.

1986, August 25: YCSD Incident Report, Case#:Y-10091-86. Victim: Ramón Ramos García.

1986, August 27: Letter from Austin L. Carroll, Corporal, Yuma County Sheriff Department to Maricopa County Organizing Project regarding Desert Deceased, Case#'s: Y-322686, Y-659286, Y-674286 Y-674486, Y-877486, Y-901286, and Y-1009186.

1987, July 20-September 1: Border Crossing/Photo Itineraries of John Annerino.

1987, October 2: USBP Tacna, AZ station. Interview of Border Patrol tracker Joe M. McCraw by John Annerino.

1987, October 2: USBP Tacna, AZ station. Interview of Border Patrol pilot David F. Roberson.

1987, December 8: Letter from Life Magazine reporter to Rosario Ruíz.

1988, February 27: Apache Jct., AZ. Author interview with Rosario Ruíz and Marcelino Ruíz regarding border crossings and bodies they encountered in desert borderlands.

1994, January 3: INS-USBP, Wellton, AZ Memorandum#:1221/61 Victim: Unidentified 64 year old male, body found.

1994, December 1: INS-USBP, Wellton, AZ Memorandum. Victim: Unidentified, body found.

1995, September 28: INS-USBP, Tucson, AZ Memorandum#:TCA1121/20 Victim: Unknown, skeletal remains found.

1996, May 15: USBP, Tucson, AZ Memorandum#: TCA 50/3.3 Victim: Unknown, woman's body found.

1996, June 14: INS-USBP, Tucson, AZ Significant Incident Report. Victim: Unknown, body of Native American found.

1996, June 29:USBP-Tucson Sector,Incident Report:TUS50/3.3C Victim: Unknown, skeletal remains found.

1996, July 1: USBP-Tucson, AZ Memorandum. Victim: Unidentified, body of woman found. [May be that of María Florencia Fermiento-Bermao of Ecuador].

1996, July 3: USBP-Tucson Sector Memorandum #: TCA 50/3.3. Victim: Enrique Montero.

1996, July 8: USBP-Tucson Sector Complaint Form #:DLG96-025. Victim: Unidentified, body found.

1998, September 14: E-mail, to Bill Broyles. Victim: Unidentified, body of Mexican man found in the Butler Mountains, Arizona.

ABBREVIATIONS USED

YCSD	Yuma County Sheriff Department
INS	Immigration and Naturalization Service
USBP	U.S. Border Patrol

INDEX

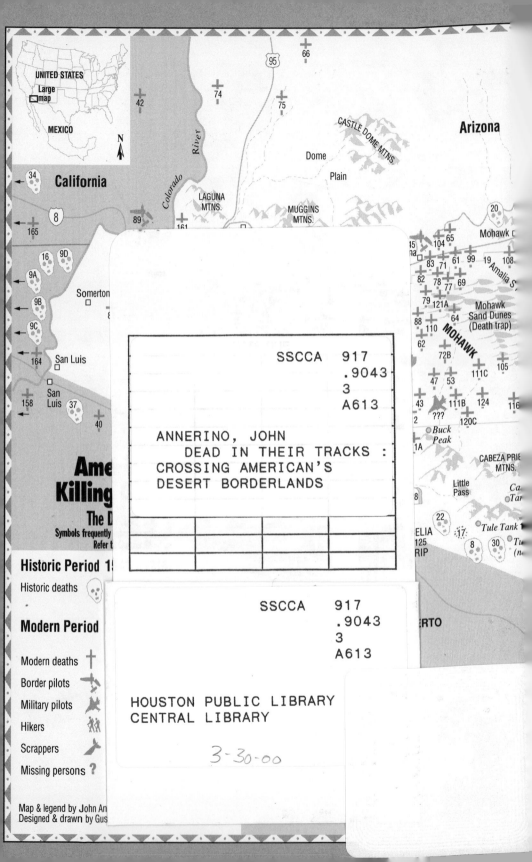

UNITED STATES
Large
map

MEXICO

N

California

Arizona

CASTLE DOME MTNS.

Dome

Plain

MUGGINS
MTNS.

LAGUNA
MTNS.

Colorado River

Mohawk

Mohawk
Sand Dunes
(Death trap)

MOHAWK

Somerton

San Luis

San
Luis

Buck
Peak

CABEZA PRIE
MTNS.

Little
Pass

Tule Tank

ELIA
RIP

PUERTO

Amalia S

Ame
Killing
The D

Symbols frequently
Refer t

Historic Period 1

Historic deaths

Modern Period

Modern deaths

Border pilots

Military pilots

Hikers

Scrappers

Missing persons ?

Map & legend by John An
Designed & drawn by Gus